BASKETBALL NOW!

BASKETBALL NOW!

THE INSIDE STORIES AND THE BRIGHTEST STARS OF THE NBA

4TH EDITION

MICHAEL GRANGE

FIREFLY BOOKS

Published by Firefly Books Ltd. 2025

First printing

Library of Congress Control Number: 2025941813

Library and Archives Canada Cataloguing in Publication
Title: Basketball now! : the inside stories and the brightest stars of the NBA / Michael Grange.
Names: Grange, Michael, author | Segal, Adam Elliott. Basketball now!
Description: 4th edition. | Previous editions written by Adam Elliott Segal, published under the title: Basketball now!: the stars and stories of the NBA.
Identifiers: Canadiana 20250235706 | ISBN 9780228105190 (softcover)
Subjects: LCSH: National Basketball Association. | LCSH: Basketball players—United States—Biography. | LCSH: Basketball players—United States. | LCSH: Basketball—United States—History. | LCGFT: Biographies.
Classification: LCC GV884.A1 S44 2025 | DDC 796.323092/273—dc23

Published in the United States by
Firefly Books (U.S.) Inc.
P.O. Box 1338, Ellicott Station
Buffalo, New York 14205

Published in Canada by
Firefly Books Ltd.
50 Staples Avenue, Unit 1
Richmond Hill, Ontario L4B 0A7

Cover and interior design: Hartley Millson

Printed in China | DC

We gratefully acknowledge the financial support of the Government of Canada for our publishing program.

Cover photo credits:
Front cover: John McCoy/Icon Sportswire
Back cover (left to right): Melissa Tamez/Icon Sportswire

Oklahoma City Thunder guard Shai Gilgeous-Alexander holds up the Finals MVP trophy as he and his teammates celebrate winning the 2025 NBA Finals on June 22, 2025.

2025 NBA FINALS MVP
NBA
CHAMPIONS
OKLAHOMA CITY
THUNDER
Champions

Jayson Tatum of the Boston Celtics reacts after scoring a three in a December 21, 2024, game against the Chicago Bulls.

CONTENTS

INTRODUCTION

What does it take to build a great team in the NBA now?

That was how I thought about the exercise of building out a roster — in book form — of the best the National Basketball Association has to offer in the present and near future.

Any good team needs a superstar or two, the kinds of players that other teams lose sleep over when thinking about how they'll try to defend them. You know, those players who provide a level of performance and consistency that sets them apart. Our opening chapter features 10 of the league's superstars, the Shai Gilgeous-Alexander and Nikola Jokic crowd. And, of course, there's still room in this section for those record-breaking league legends — Stephen Curry, Kevin Durant, LeBron James — who've remained elite decades into their careers.

Then you have the "game changers": they are top players, often good enough to lead teams on their own. Say hello to your Tyrese Haliburtons and Jimmy Butlers, your Kawhi Leonards and your Donovan Mitchells (and others). Any franchise would love to have them, and the winning ones usually do.

Of course, teams can't win at the highest level without playing elite defense, and the NBA now has a deep roster of great individual and team defenders. I've compiled a list of 10 of them — Luguentz Dort, Draymond Green, Rudy Gobert and others — who do it better than anyone else. These are the players who love chasing down balls, blocking shots and generally making a scorer's life miserable.

The league is constantly being replenished by emerging young talent, and if a team has Victor Wembanyama, Amen Thompson, Paolo Banchero or Jalen Williams on the roster, it's probably in a good spot. This chapter features the rising stars — the young players with considerable raw talent who, in a few years' time, may become the next set of superstars and game changers.

And finally, there are players who could fit in one or another category but are mainly just gifted athletes who help their teams win games. They are the winners, like Aaron Gordon, Al Horford and Jalen Brunson, and we have a category for them, too.

But all of that requires context, and so the essays about the end of the LeBron-KD-Steph era, the league's shift to parity, the influx of international players and the rising importance of the three-point shot are an effort to provide a screen grab of the ever-changing NBA game as it stands *now*. Enjoy!

— Michael Grange, July 2025

Superstars square up at the NBA All-Star Game on February 16, 2025, in San Francisco. Stephen Curry of Shaq's OGs defends Shai Gilgeous-Alexander of Chuck's Global Stars at the annual NBA gala. Choosing a roster for this book often felt a lot like building the teams for the All-Star weekend.

ALL
STAR

SUPERSTARS

Giannis Antetokounmpo

MILWAUKEE BUCKS

34 Giannis ANTETOKOUNMPO

POSITION PF, SF, PG, SG // **SHOOTS** RIGHT // **HEIGHT** 6'11" // **WEIGHT** 242 LBS // **DRAFTED** 2013, 15TH OVERALL

The higher you climb, the steeper it gets.

For Giannis Antetokounmpo, the final steps toward basketball immortality have been steep, with no shortage of stumbles.

The unlikely Milwaukee Bucks superstar long ago cemented himself as an all-time NBA great. The gangly prospect, taken 15th overall in the 2013 draft, built his career in rapid increments, reaching the peak of the basketball world in summer 2021, when, as a two-time regular-season MVP, he led the Bucks to their first league title in 50 years, earning Finals MVP honors along the way.

His status in NBA history is unassailable. The list of players who have amassed his levels of statistical production while leading teams to a title is short.

Since earning his first MVP award in 2018–19, Antetokounmpo has averaged 29.6 points, 12 rebounds and 6 assists per game, while converting on 57.5 percent of his field goal attempts over seven seasons. For context, only three-time MVP Nikola Jokic has even had a single season with averages of at least 29/12/6 on 57.5 percent shooting. Over that span the Bucks star has won the MVP award twice and finished in the top four of MVP voting every year. For his career he's been named to the All-NBA team nine times (every year since 2016–17) and to the All-Defensive team four times. In fact, Antetokounmpo won Defensive Player of the Year in 2020–21, joining Michael Jordan as the only players to win multiple MVPs and earn recognition as the league's best defender.

His individual and team accomplishments have been the headline on a remarkable personal success story. The middle son of five athletic brothers, Antetokounmpo was born in Greece to Nigerian immigrant parents who struggled to scratch out a living in Athens. He was convinced to try basketball after a scout for a small local club spotted

CAREER HIGHLIGHTS

- > 2020–21 NBA Champion
- > 2-time MVP (2018–19, 2019–20)
- > 2021 All-Star Game MVP
- > 2019–20 Defensive Player of the Year
- > 9-time All Star

Giannis Antetokounmpo drives to the basket past Victor Wembanyama of the San Antonio Spurs in a game on January 31, 2025.

the exceptionally tall, lanky teenager playing street soccer. At first he and his older brother Thanasis (later drafted by the New York Knicks and eventually a teammate on the Bucks) had to share a pair of shoes, taking turns playing while the other watched. On other occasions they would miss practices because they needed to help their family by working as street vendors.

"Sometimes our fridge was empty," Antetokounmpo told *The New York Times*. "Some days, we didn't sell the stuff, and we didn't have money to feed ourselves."

Perhaps that helps explain both Antetokounmpo's determined style of play — few NBA role players, let alone superstars, play as consistently hard — and his well-rounded perspective.

Even at his peak, Antetokounmpo's team fell short of the expectations his individual greatness created. The Bucks emerged as perennial title contenders in 2018–19, when they won 60 games and Antetokounmpo won the first of his back-to-back MVP awards. But over the next six seasons they made the NBA Finals just once. Three times they lost in the first round and twice in the second round.

"Every year you work, you work toward something, toward a goal, right? Which is to get a promotion, be able to take care of your family, to be able to provide the house for them or take care of your parents," Antetokounmpo said after the Bucks were eliminated in the first round of the 2022–23 playoffs. He had just been asked if their 58-win season had been a failure because of their early exit. "You work toward a goal. It's not a failure; it's steps to success.

"Michael Jordan played 15 years, won six championships; the other nine years was a failure? That's what you're telling me? There's no failure in sports. You know, there's good days, bad days. Some days you are able to be successful, some days you're not. Some days it's your turn, some days it's not your turn. And that's what sports is about. You don't always win; some other team's gonna win. And this year, somebody else is gonna win. Simple as that."

The following 2023–24 season wasn't much better. Even after Milwaukee's dramatic move to acquire Portland Trail Blazers superstar Damian Lillard to pair with Antetokounmpo, the results didn't follow, as the Bucks won just 49 games — their lowest regular-season total since 2017–18, Antetokounmpo's fifth season. The Bucks star delivered, as always, averaging 30.4 points, 11.5 rebounds and 6.5 assists and finishing fourth in the MVP voting while earning All-NBA First Team honors for the sixth-straight season. But in the playoffs he was hampered by a strained calf and played in only three games as the Bucks fell in six to the Indiana Pacers.

The hope was 2024–25 would be different, but it played out as so many years have outside the Bucks' championship season: incredible individual production but stumbling when it comes to team success. Antetokounmpo averaged 30.4 points, 11.9 rebounds and 6.5 assists on 60.1 percent shooting and finished third in the MVP voting, but the Bucks were eliminated in the first round by the Indiana Pacers — this time with Lillard going down with an injury.

Antetokounmpo's story is an inspiration, and his Hall-of-Fame credentials are beyond doubt. The only question is if he can win another championship in Milwaukee, or if he'll have to take his one-of-a-kind talent elsewhere to achieve yet another improbable dream. ■

PHOENIX SUNS

Devin BOOKER

POSITION SG, PG // **SHOOTS** RIGHT // **HEIGHT** 6'6" // **WEIGHT** 206 LBS // **DRAFTED** 2015, 13TH OVERALL

Devin Booker wasn't projected to be an NBA superstar; not all that many players taken 13th overall in the draft ever reach that exalted level.

But the Phoenix Suns guard became one, announcing his intentions when, as a 20-year-old in his second season, he went off for 71 points against the Boston Celtics, on March 24, 2017 — in Boston, it's worth noting. Booker became just the sixth player in league history to top the 70-point mark. The rest you may have heard of: Wilt Chamberlain, Elgin Baylor, David Thompson, David Robinson and Kobe Bryant. For context, Kareem Abdul-Jabbar never scored 70 in a game even though he held the NBA's all-time scoring record for 39 years. Michael Jordan averaged 37 points a season once — the highest by anyone other than Chamberlain — and his single-game best was 69 points. LeBron James broke Abdul-Jabbar's all-time record without scoring 60 points in a game even once.

By his fourth season Booker was undeniably one of the best players at his position as he joined Oscar Robertson and James as the only players in league history to average at least 26.6 points and 6.8 assists before their age-23 season. But since the Suns averaged just 22 wins per year over that stretch, he didn't get the recognition his performance deserved.

Ironically, Booker's path to full-blown appreciation came by being ready and willing to relinquish some of the perks of NBA superstardom and signing on to become an elite role player on Team USA at the 2024 Olympics.

The year before, the powerhouse Americans had come home from the 2023 FIBA Basketball World Cup with their tails between their legs and a disappointing fourth-place finish. Then-Washington Wizards forward Kyle Kuzma said out loud what many were thinking when he took to social media: "USA basketball better get some nba stars that know how to play a role. Anybody can be nice with the ball in their hands but can you be cool with defending and going to the corner for a few possessions?"

To which Booker, already a gold medalist after playing for Team USA at the 2020 Olympics, responded, "I'll do it."

He was a man of his word. Team USA's 2024 Olympic team was loaded with generational superstars, the team's identity crafted around LeBron James,

Devin Booker shoots over Jalen Duren of the Detroit Pistons on January 18, 2025, in Detroit.

CAREER HIGHLIGHTS

- 4-time All Star
- 2021–22 All-NBA First Team
- 2023–24 All-NBA Third Team
- 2015–16 All-Rookie Team

Kevin Durant and Stephen Curry, with either Anthony Davis or Joel Embiid patrolling the middle. Booker carved out a starting spot by playing a role substantially different than what his day job with the Suns requires, playing off the ball, being ready to catch-and-shoot when the chances came and setting the tone defensively.

It paid off brilliantly. Booker had Team USA's highest cumulative plus-minus, started every game, shot a blistering 57 percent from beyond the arc to lead the team and was tops in the tournament in assist-to-turnover ratio.

By fitting in with the biggest stars on the biggest stage, Booker stood out.

"Devin Booker is an incredible basketball player," Team USA head coach Steve Kerr said after his team's Olympic gold-medal win over France. "Nobody asked about him [but he] was our unsung MVP. I just wanted to say that."

That Booker was a cornerstone piece on a winning team is no surprise. When the Suns added Hall of Fame–bound point guard Chris Paul for the 2020–21 season to lend some veteran heft to a rising young team, it was all the help Booker needed to prove that the losing years he'd gone through early in his career were merely a product of circumstance.

After posting the league's second-best regular-season record in 2020–21, the Suns advanced all the way to the 2021 NBA Finals before losing in six games to the Milwaukee Bucks.

Booker looked every inch a playoff veteran. In his playoff debut Booker scored 34 points and added 7 rebounds and 8 assists in a series-opening win over the defending NBA champion Los Angeles Lakers. In Game 6 Booker scored 47 points to eliminate them. After a four-game sweep of the Denver Nuggets in the second round, Booker recorded the first triple-double of his career — 40 points, 13 rebounds and 11 assists — in Game 1 of the Western Conference Finals, a win over the Los Angeles Clippers. By the time the Suns' run was over, Booker had set a new NBA record for points scored in a playoff debut — 601 — and cemented himself as one of the most complete players in the league.

"Everything he's doing now … we knew, we just knew," said then-Bucks forward and former Suns teammate P.J. Tucker of Booker's postseason breakout. "And when you've been around and played against a bunch of guys, in this fraternity, we all know each other. We all played against each other. We all knew that he was going to be really good. Like he wasn't just good, he was really good … he showed that he was one of the ones. He just like took it, and he just elevated. He became who he is and who he's continuing to be."

The Suns tried to build on that success, but chasing championships is an uncertain business. After Phoenix added Kevin Durant and Bradley Beal in "win now" moves before the 2023–24 season, injuries, lack of depth and poor chemistry held the Suns back from reaching their potential. Booker, as always, did his part, joining three-time MVP Nikola Jokic as the only players in the NBA to average at least 26 points and 7 assists per game with a True Shooting percentage of 60 percent or better over 2023–24 and 2024–25. ■

30 Stephen CURRY

POSITION PG // **SHOOTS** RIGHT // **HEIGHT** 6'2" // **WEIGHT** 185 LBS // **DRAFTED** 2009, 7TH OVERALL

On top of everything else Stephen Curry can do, he can speak French.

Well, he at least knows how to translate his signature "night, night" gesture, where he puts two hands together to the side of his face — the universal sign that it's time for bed, or in this case, it's game over. The Golden State Warriors legend has been delivering it late in NBA games for years, typically after he hits a flurry of three-pointers, ending any hopes of victory for his opponent.

There is almost nothing Curry hasn't done on an NBA floor, as a four-time champion, a two-time regular-season MVP, the 2022 Finals MVP and the most accomplished shooter in basketball history. One of the few gaps on his Hall-of-Fame résumé was an Olympic gold medal, but Curry fixed that in his first chance, when he started for Team USA at the 2024 Olympic Games in Paris.

First Curry helped propel USA into the gold-medal game with a 36-point explosion against Serbia in a riveting semifinal, and then — fittingly — Curry helped put the American powerhouse over the top with an avalanche of four triples in the last 2:45 of the final against host France. After his finishing dagger — a step-back over two defenders — Curry jogged back up the floor and signaled "night, night" to the crowd. For good measure, after the game Curry put on a hoodie with the words "nuit, nuit" (French for "night, night") and the Eiffel Tower across his chest.

Curry had his gold medal and another unforgettable moment in a career filled with them.

"A big shot to put us up six. That kind of settled everything," Curry said of his late-game firestorm. "And then the rhythm, the avalanche came, and thankfully the other three went in. That was an unbelievable moment. I've been blessed to play basketball at a high level for a very long time. This ranks very high in terms of excitement and the sense of relief, getting to the finish line."

Curry has rarely faltered when the stakes are at their highest. Whether it's in France, starring for his country, or in Boston, helping lift the Warriors to their fourth championship by dropping his Finals-best 43 points on the Celtics in Game 4 of the 2022 NBA Finals, he finds a way to make his mark.

He's got the gold medal and the 2022 Finals MVP award to prove it.

Curry's legend was already secure

even without his long list of big-game heroics. In the big picture, there are few players in NBA history who have had a greater impact on the sport, even if no one saw it coming when he was drafted seventh overall by Golden State after a prolific three-year college career at Davidson.

But Curry's trademark attribute — the ability to shoot from distance in almost any circumstance — became weaponized by the Warriors, especially once Steve Kerr took over as head coach in 2014–15 and guided the Warriors to a 67-win season and the franchise's first championship. Curry won the first of his MVP awards that year, launching 646 threes and making 283, for a 44.5 percent conversion rate.

But Curry was just getting warmed up. The following season he made 402 threes — which remains the single-season record — at 45.4 percent, the best accuracy mark ever for someone with at least 450 attempts, on his way to his second MVP award.

Overall, his 2015–16 campaign — 30.1 points, 6.7 assists, a league-leading 2.1 steals per game — stands as one of the best individual seasons in league history. Only Kareem Abdul-Jabbar, Wilt Chamberlain, Michael Jordan and LeBron James have a Win Shares per 48-minute mark better than Curry's .318 that year.

Curry broke the career record of 2,973 made threes held by Ray Allen midway through the 2021–22 season. By the end of the 2024–25 season, Curry pushed the figure to 4,058. Five thousand sounds doable if he plays until he's 40, which doesn't seem out of the question given that Curry was named to an All-NBA team for the 11th time in the season that he turned 37. His record could end up being one of the most untouchable marks in all of sports.

"I don't think there's anybody in sight now that can break his record," said Dirk Nowitzki, one of the greatest shooting big men in NBA history. "[Steph] changed the game. He makes it look too easy. He's the best shooter I've ever seen, and I think it's clear he is the best catch-and-shoot player, but where he's so good is off the dribble, and I think that's something he added — the quick three off the dribble. It's one motion, and his shot is gone."

Curry's fingerprint on basketball history will remain. His flare for the dramatic is almost as impressive.

Stephen Curry goes for a layup against the Washington Wizards defense in a January 18, 2025, game in San Francisco.

CAREER HIGHLIGHTS

- 4-time NBA Champion (2014–15, 2016–17, 2017–18, 2021–22)
- 2-time MVP (2014–15, 2015–16)
- 2021–22 Finals MVP
- 2021–22 Western Conference Finals MVP
- 2-time All-Star Game MVP (2022, 2025)

LOS ANGELES LAKERS

77

Luka DONCIC

POSITION PG, SG // **SHOOTS** RIGHT // **HEIGHT** 6'6" // **WEIGHT** 230 LBS // **DRAFTED** 2018, 3RD OVERALL

Unprecedented.

There are countless adjectives and superlatives that can be used to capture the unfolding greatness of Luka Doncic, the giant point guard starring for the Los Angeles Lakers. But perhaps the best place to begin is where the comparisons stop.

Sure, Doncic shares traits with some of the greatest to ever step on a basketball floor — LeBron James, Magic Johnson, Larry Bird and Oscar Robertson are all first-ballot Hall of Famers whose brilliance gets referenced when trying to convey how the Slovenian can dominate games and bend defenses.

But he's separated himself from even their hallowed standard by how good he has been so early in his NBA career, and how consistent he's been in his greatness.

No other player in league history has ever, for example, accumulated five All-NBA First Team nominations and a Rookie of the Year award by the time they were 25.

No one has ever boasted career averages of at least 28 points, 8.6 rebounds and 8.2 assists a game through their first seven seasons. The 82 triple-doubles he collected through the end of his seventh season ranks him seventh all-time, and he is the first player to collect 80 triple-doubles before his 26th birthday since the NBA–ABA merger in 1976.

It's why, when coaches and players with years of perspective try to capture the impact Doncic has had since breaking into the NBA in 2018, the comparisons are with the best of the best.

"I hesitate to throw out names like LeBron James and Magic Johnson, who have been do-everything kind of stars," said then-Mavericks head coach Rick Carlisle during Doncic's second season, when he led Dallas to the playoffs for the first time. "But it's pretty clear now that Luka has many of those same traits and has proven that he can do a lot of those things. He has deceptive size, strength and quickness — and an understanding beyond his years on how to use his body to make plays and draw fouls."

Doncic has always had all the qualities required for generational excellence. At 6-foot-6 and 230 pounds, he has tremendous size for his position, and his combination of shooting and passing ability, combined with his determination to play the game at his pace, means he can dictate the game one possession at a time. Crowd him

CAREER HIGHLIGHTS

- 2023–24 Western Conference Finals MVP
- 2018–19 Rookie of the Year
- 5-time All Star
- 5-time All-NBA First Team

and he's in the paint, ready to score or draw fouls. Give him room and he can settle into threes with unlimited range. Commit multiple defenders and he'll thread bullet-like passes to open shooters or toss lobs to the rim.

"I feel like I want to be the hero of the game, you know?" Doncic told ESPN.com the year before he was eligible to join the NBA. "Every time, I wanted the ball in my hands, from the very beginning. I have missed some important shots before, but you need to learn from this. You need to move on. If you have a nice game or a bad game, you will have a thousand more games."

His peers recognized his gifts when Doncic was a teenager and see the same qualities on display on the world's biggest stage now.

"When we used to play video games, he's the same guy. He's really competitive," said Spanish international Juancho Hernangomez, who has been friends with Doncic since they were training for professional careers in Spain. "When [he] catches fire, he's tough to guard. He's got God's gift of talent, God has given it to him, and you know he's going to make the last shot and gonna do tricky shots, shoot it from half court and make it [to win]. That's how he is.

"If someone can do that, it is him."

Regardless of the situation, Doncic's ability to impose his will on games never seems to waver. It was present when he signed his first professional contract with European powerhouse Real Madrid as a 13-year-old and when he led the club to the EuroLeague championship as an 18-year-old, earning MVP honors for both the regular season and the championship finals along the way — the youngest to ever manage that feat. It was present when Doncic averaged 31 points, 9.8 rebounds and 8.7 assists in his first NBA playoff series at age 20. It was on full display when he scored 36 points on 14-of-22 shooting on the way to eliminating Minnesota in the Western Conference Finals in 2024, lifting the Mavericks to the NBA Finals for the first time since 2011.

The will to win at the highest level and the ability to make it happen have always been part of his DNA, and given his age, his impact has only begun. He set the NBA on its ear when he was traded to the Los Angeles Lakers in February 2025, a deal that no one saw coming given Doncic's stature in Dallas. Other than then-three-time MVP Kareem Abdul-Jabbar being traded from the Milwaukee Bucks to the Lakers in the summer of 1975, there may not have been a better player traded at that stage of their career. The midseason deal joined Doncic in his prime with the last great years of LeBron James.

Luka Doncic shoots over Houston Rockets guard Fred VanVleet on March 31, 2025, in Los Angeles.

No one was happier about the trade than his new teammate: "[Doncic] plays the game how I always wanted to inspire the next generation to play the game," James said on his *Mind the Game* podcast with Steve Nash. "There's nothing predetermined. If you have two guys on you, there's a numbers game. If you have the advantage and there's a guy that can't guard you or you're able to beat him … I'm able to make the passes or make the reads before they happen. I've always loved the players that breathe so much confidence into his teammates, that make them believe that they're actually better than what [they] really are … Luka has done that for seven years."

And now likely will for many more in Los Angeles. ■

HOUSTON ROCKETS

POSITION SF, PF, SG // **SHOOTS** RIGHT // **HEIGHT** 6'11" // **WEIGHT** 240 LBS // **DRAFTED** 2007, 2ND OVERALL

When will Kevin Durant stop being great?

Never, maybe? The NBA veteran is the league's original unicorn. In a sport filled with one-in-a-million marvels, Durant has been a rarity from the moment he stepped on the floor for the first time with the Seattle SuperSonics, after being the No. 2 pick in the 2007 draft. He averaged 20.1 points a game as a teenaged rookie, and at 21 he won the first of his four scoring titles when he put up 30.1 points a game after the SuperSonics had relocated to Oklahoma City.

The singular excellence has never stopped. In 2023–24, at age 35, in his 16th season, he put up one of the best seasons of his career. He averaged 27.1 points, 6.6 rebounds, 5 assists and 1.2 blocks over 75 games with the Phoenix Suns on mind-boggling efficiency, as Durant converted 56.7 percent of his two-point field goals, shot 41.3 percent from three on more than five attempts per game and shot 85.6 percent from the line.

It was a resounding answer to anyone who questioned — after injuries had limited Durant to just 137 games over the previous four seasons — if time had finally passed by the 11-time All-NBA selection.

Not at all, it turns out. And just for good measure, Durant joined forces with fellow graybeards Stephen Curry and LeBron James to bring home Olympic gold from Paris in 2024, the fourth time the former University of Texas star had won gold with Team USA, becoming Team USA's all-time leading scorer in the process.

A lot has changed in the basketball world since Durant broke in, but the same set of facts are as true now as ever.

Doc Rivers has more than 2,700 NBA games of experience as a player and head coach in a career that spans more than 40 years, and he got it right when assessing Durant during the 2011–12 season, when Durant was on his way to his third scoring title.

Kevin Durant, playing for the Phoenix Suns, drives to the basket on Denver Nuggets forward Peyton Watson during a December 25, 2024, game.

CAREER HIGHLIGHTS

- 2-time NBA Champion (2016–17, 2017–18)
- 2013–14 MVP
- 2-time Finals MVP (2016–17, 2017–18)
- 2-time All-Star Game MVP (2012, 2019)
- 15-time All Star

"I don't think there's been a Kevin Durant. Ever," said Rivers. "I don't think there's ever been a comparison ... He's 7 feet tall and he's running around like a two-guard. He can handle the ball, he can take you off the dribble, he can post you up, he shoots over you. You can't trap him because he sees right over you. I don't think in the years that I've coached and played ... there's ever been a more difficult guy to prepare for."

Durant has proven Rivers correct over and over again. After his prolific nine-season tenure with the Oklahoma City Thunder, which included a run to the 2012 NBA Finals, Durant rocked the basketball world by choosing to join the Golden State Warriors in 2016–17, as they were coming off their record-setting 73-win season and Finals loss in 2015–16.

It seemed like an embarrassment of riches for the Warriors, who were adding — arguably — the NBA's best offensive player to a franchise that was reshaping how offense was being played. Durant took some criticism for front-running, but he shook that off as easily as he has any All-NBA defender over his career.

"We live in this superhero comic book world where either you're a villain or you're a superhero if you're in this position, and I know that, and I know I haven't changed as a person," he said. "I don't treat people any differently because I made the decision to play basketball in another city. I understand the fans in Oklahoma City and basketball fans around the world are, I guess, upset. But like I said, I made the decision based upon what I wanted to do and how I felt, and it's the best decision for me, so I can't really control how you feel."

He remained in complete control of his game. In sparking the Warriors to consecutive titles, Durant was twice named Finals MVP. He very likely would have led the Warriors to three-straight titles were it not for an Achilles tendon injury suffered in the 2019 Finals that would keep him out for all of the 2019–20 season. Over 47 playoff games with the Warriors, Durant averaged 29.6 points, 7.1 rebounds and 4.5 assists with 50/40/90 shooting splits from the field, the three-point line and the free-throw line.

Durant's story continued from there, although injuries prevented him from tasting a championship during his two years in Brooklyn with the Nets and his two with the Suns. Durant was traded to the Houston Rockets in the 2025 offseason, a deal that saw him land in Texas in exchange for Dillon Brooks, Jalen Green and six draft picks.

While more rings have eluded him to this point, as one of the most potent offensive forces of his or any generation, he has proven at every step in his Hall of Fame–bound career that his greatness has yet to find its limit. ■

21

Joel EMBIID

POSITION C // **SHOOTS** RIGHT // **HEIGHT** 7'0" // **WEIGHT** 280 LBS // **DRAFTED** 2014, 3RD OVERALL

The greater your potential, the harder it is to reach it.

That's become the defining challenge of Joel Embiid's career. The Philadelphia 76ers star has shown that he is, at his best, the most singularly dominant player in the NBA. At times he's demonstrated that he could or should be counted among the very best to have ever stepped foot on an NBA court.

But those times have been too few and far between as the giant center — who can wow with his finesse on one play and overwhelm opponents with his size and power on the next — has struggled with injury and inconsistency at various points throughout his first decade in the NBA. No one doubts that Embiid is capable of almost anything he wants on the basketball floor; the only questions are if and when.

Embiid put most of those issues to rest over a three-year stretch, beginning with the pandemic-shortened 2020–21 season, when was healthy enough to play in 78 percent of the Sixers' games and delivered numbers worthy of a Hall of Famer.

From 2020–21 to 2022–23, Embiid averaged 30.9 points, 10.8 rebounds, 3.8 assists and 1.5 blocked shots. He reliably stepped outside and made threes (converting 1.2 per game), was lethal in the midrange as he made 50 percent of his jumpers from 10 feet to the three-point line, and bullied his way to the free-throw line nearly 11.5 times a game, making 84.2 percent of those chances.

He can shoot over the defense, drive around them or simply use his 7-foot, 280-pound frame to overpower the opposition near the basket.

"At the end, that's what makes me unguardable," Embiid told reporters in early 2021. "If you're gonna crowd me, I'm gonna find my way to the free-throw line, or I'm gonna end up at the basket. And if you're gonna back up on me. I got that hesitation shot, and I also got my favorite, just a pull-up shot, or just the easy shot that I always get in the post."

CAREER HIGHLIGHTS

- > 2022–23 MVP
- > 7-time All Star
- > 2022–23 All-NBA First Team
- > 4-time All-NBA Second Team
- > 3-time All-Defensive Second Team

Embiid finished second in MVP voting to Nikola Jokic, another prolific big man, in 2021 and 2022, but in 2023 he won the award, along with the NBA scoring title — validation for a career that seemed like it was bound to generate multiple awards but was so often undone by injuries.

"I know I've always said I don't care, but it was just for you guys [the media] to leave me alone," the gifted center said after he was voted to his first MVP. "I do care in the way that it validates everything, all the work that you've put in. And to be sitting here is just amazing."

The MVP win was another improbable step for one of the NBA's most improbable stars. A soccer and volleyball player growing up in Yaoundé, Cameroon, Embiid only started playing basketball at age 15. He moved to the United States for high school at 16, earned a scholarship to Kansas two years later, and after his fourth season of basketball was the No. 3 pick in the 2014 draft. Foot injuries delayed his NBA debut for two full seasons and in his third he only played 31 games due to a knee injury. But there was never any doubt of his talent. In just his 43rd career game Embiid put up 46 points while grabbing 15 rebounds and counting 7 blocks and 7 assists in a win over the Los Angeles Lakers, becoming the only player to have a 46-15-7-7 line since the NBA began tracking blocked shots in 1983–84.

With health came accomplishments: consecutive scoring titles in 2021–22 and 2022–23 and his MVP

Joel Embiid scores against the Toronto Raptors on February 11, 2025, in Philadelphia.

award in 2022–23. Embiid was well on his way to another MVP in 2023–24. He was averaging a league-leading 34.7 points a game at the midway point of the season, joining Wilt Chamberlain as the only players in league history to average more than a point per minute played (Embiid averaged 33.6 minutes played). But once more injuries interrupted his progress, this time a bone bruise in his left knee.

Embiid made it back for the playoffs, but the Sixers lost to the New York Knicks in the first round — his own effectiveness limited after a long layoff and a knee that required a bulky brace. Unfortunately for Embiid, the 76ers and basketball fans everywhere, the injury bug followed him into the 2024–25 season — a year that began with significant promise with the addition of nine-time All Star Paul George in free agency. Instead of competing for a championship, Embiid's season ended after a career-low 19 games, with his troublesome knee requiring surgery.

This has been the story of his star-crossed career. He's delivered on all his promises: at his best he's one of the greats, with a 70-point game on his résumé as well as All-Star nominations, All-NBA recognition and a regular spot at or near the top of the league's MVP voting.

But he's never been able to lift the Sixers past the second round of the playoffs — let alone lift the championship trophy — and his uncertain health has been a big reason why.

OKLAHOMA CITY THUNDER

2 Shai GILGEOUS-ALEXANDER

POSITION PG, SG // **SHOOTS** RIGHT // **HEIGHT** 6'6" // **WEIGHT** 200 LBS // **DRAFTED** 2018, 11TH OVERALL

Everyday greatness is what superstars are made of, which goes a long way toward explaining how Shai Gilgeous-Alexander went from "interesting young player" to must-watch in the space of three NBA seasons.

"I'm very, very strict on consistency in every aspect of life," Gilgeous-Alexander said midway through 2023–24, when his play and the Oklahoma City Thunder's rise had pushed him to the forefront of the league's MVP race in his sixth season. "And I think it helps my basketball. Whether it's my eating, my day-to-day schedule, how clean my house is. It's what I do with my time, whether I'm playing or not. I try to be very, very strict on discipline, being consistent."

It's not flashy, but consistency works, and Gilgeous-Alexander's steady rise has been about getting incrementally better to the point where his greatness can't be ignored.

Gilgeous-Alexander is long and lanky, and instead of dominating with explosive athleticism, he uses a combination of quickness, timing and skill to keep entire defenses off balance and get to the paint at will, where he is among the most effective finishers in the game.

"He's just so dynamic," said NBA veteran Kelly Olynyk, who played with Gilgeous-Alexander as they helped the Canadian men's national team to a bronze medal at the FIBA Basketball World Cup in 2023. "The thing about Shai is that ... everything is so effortless and so easy. He's so smooth, you can't speed him up and he just gets things done; he makes plays in big moments. He's always alive, you can't rest or break, ever, when you're guarding him. It's tough."

The best players in the sport are usually fully visible for years before they realize their destiny. LeBron James was famously on the cover of *Sports Illustrated* when he was 17 years old. Kevin Durant was scoring by the boatload at the University of Texas before he was the second pick in the 2007 draft.

But even when Gilgeous-Alexander arrived at the University of Kentucky as a freshman, no one was projecting stardom. Initially he wasn't even supposed to start for then-head coach John Calipari. He showed enough in leading the Wildcats to the Sweet 16 in 2018 that the Los Angeles Clippers drafted him 11th overall that same year. He had a nice first season — he made the All-Rookie Second Team — but few were focused on Gilgeous-Alexander being included in the trade with Oklahoma City for Paul George in the summer of 2019.

Shai Gilgeous-Alexander shoots over his cousin Nickeil Alexander-Walker of the Minnesota Timberwolves in Game 1 of the Western Conference Finals on May 20, 2025.

CAREER HIGHLIGHTS

- 2024–25 NBA Champion
- 2024–25 MVP
- 2024–25 NBA Finals MVP
- 3-time All Star
- 3-time All-NBA First Team

In OKC, Gilgeous-Alexander made solid progress from his rookie season, but he was overshadowed by Chris Paul on a feisty Thunder team that unexpectedly made the playoffs.

And then the Thunder went deep into rebuilding. Gilgeous-Alexander averaged then-career highs of 23.7 points in his third season and 24.5 in his fourth, but he did it while being limited to 35 and 56 games due to injury. All the while the Thunder won just 22 and 24 games those seasons, which kept his budding stardom largely under wraps.

That's all changed now. The 6-foot-6 guard from Hamilton, Ontario, broke out in his fifth season in 2022–23, as he exploded for 31.4 points a game to go along with 4.8 rebounds and 5.5 assists while also contributing 1.6 steals and a block per game. He earned All-NBA First Team honors and finished fifth in MVP voting as the Thunder jumped to 40 wins and earned a spot in the Play-in Tournament, exceeding all expectations.

In 2023–24 he had a "break-in" season, as in, he broke into the conversation about who the best players in the NBA are and will be.

He averaged more than 30 points a game (30.1) for the second-straight season, grabbed more rebounds (5.5), dished more assists (6.2) and averaged the most steals on his team, which won 57 games and earned the first seed in the Western Conference. He became one of five players in league history — MVP winners Michael Jordan, Stephen Curry, James Harden and Rick Barry — to record a 30/6/5/2 season, and trailed only Curry's epic 2015–16 performance in terms of scoring efficiency. Along the way he broke Kevin Durant's franchise record for most 30-point games in a season with 51 — only 10 other players in league history have ever had more in a single season, all of them Hall of Famers or, in the case of Harden, headed there.

The 2024–25 season demonstrated what Gilgeous-Alexander has been working toward as he put up a career-high 32.7 points to win his first scoring title, while adding a career-best 6.4 assists along with 5 rebounds, 1.7 steals and a blocked shot per game. His ability to combine volume scoring with efficiency, playmaking and defensive activity is almost unmatched. The OKC star joined Jordan as the only players in league history to average at least 30 points, 6 assists, 1.5 steals and 1 block per game with a True Shooting percentage of .600 or better. That he did all of that while helping the Thunder to a league-leading 68-14 record made Gilgeous-Alexander an easy choice to win his first MVP award and, after leading OKC to its first championship as the Thunder, his first Finals MVP award. He joined all-time greats Kareem Abdul-Jabbar, Jordan and Shaquille O'Neal as the only players to win the scoring title, the regular-season MVP and the Finals MVP in the same season.

"It's hard to believe that I'm part of that group," he said after averaging 30.3 points, 5.6 assists, 1.9 steals and 1.6 blocks in the Thunder's seven-game series win over the Indiana Pacers. "It's hard to even fathom that I'm that type of basketball player sometimes.

"As a kid, you dream ... But you don't ever really know if it's going to come true. I'm just glad and happy that my dreams have been able to come true." ■

LOS ANGELES LAKERS

23 LeBron JAMES

POSITION SF, PF, PG, SG // **SHOOTS** RIGHT // **HEIGHT** 6'9" // **WEIGHT** 250 LBS // **DRAFTED** 2003, 1ST OVERALL

There may never be a day when NBA fans are completely done with debating who is the GOAT, the greatest of all time.

The front runners are almost always LeBron James and Michael Jordan, though arguments can be made for the likes of Kareem Abdul-Jabbar (six MVPs, six NBA championships), Bill Russell (11 NBA titles) or Wilt Chamberlain (the NBA record book will explain why).

But there is no question about who has been the greatest for the longest. No NBA player has been as dominant as James has for as long as he has. This may also be true across all sports. Finding a major athlete who has been among the very best on the planet across two decades is nearly impossible.

As a point of comparison, consider this: When James broke Abdul-Jabbar's all-time scoring record with a trademark fadeaway jumper from the elbow on February 7, 2023, it was a milestone achieved during yet another All-NBA season, in which he averaged 29.3 points, 8.4 rebounds and 6.9 assists per 36 minutes at the age of 38. How impressive is that?

When James was at his absolute peak more than a decade earlier, winning four MVP awards in five seasons from 2008–09 through 2012–13, he averaged "just" 26.2 points, 7.2 rebounds and 6.9 assists on a per-36-minutes basis.

Meanwhile, Jordan's age-38 season was his second-last, and while it was impressive — he averaged 22.9 points, 5.7 rebounds, 5.2 assists and 1.4 steals while being named an All Star for

LeBron James dunks in a February 22, 2025, game against the Denver Nuggets.

the 13th time — he shot a career-low 41.6 percent from the floor and was a shadow of the athletic marvel who had won the last of his six MVP awards four years earlier, at age 34.

Similarly, when Abdul-Jabbar set the scoring record following the 1988–89 season, he was still a contributing player at age 41, but he was three years removed from being an All-NBA player, and his averages of 10.1 points, 4.5 rebounds and 1.1 blocks in 22.9 minutes were all career lows.

LeBron, in contrast to even his few contemporaries among NBA greats, shows no sign of slowing down.

"I give myself an opportunity to, I guess, surprise myself still what I'm able to do for as long as I've been in this league and for as many miles as I've put on these tires," James said as he worked his way to his NBA-record 20th (and counting) All-NBA selection in 2023–24, his 21st season. "I wanna continue to defy the odds, continue to have this battle with Father Time that for so long everybody said has been undefeated ... [I'm] trying to give him one loss."

James has been so good for so long that in 2024–25 he became the first player in NBA history to take the court with his son, LeBron "Bronny" James Jr., who was taken with the 55th pick in the 2024 draft by the Lakers.

It's another milestone in a career full of them for the player who was put on the cover of *Sports Illustrated* as a 17-year-old high school junior with the headline "The Chosen One" and then proceeded to exceed even the most hyperbolic expectations.

Nobody knows when James will finally retire — he's under contract through the 2025–26 season at least — but when he does, he'll likely have a hold on the all-time NBA record book that will almost be impossible for anyone to match.

He's already the first NBA player to reach 40,000 points — only seven other players had crossed the 30,000-point threshold by the end of the 2024–25 season and only one, Kevin Durant, is an active player. James also ranks fourth in assists, sixth in steals and 25th in total rebounds. Presuming he plays out his contract, he'll also retire as the NBA's career leader in seasons, games and minutes played.

And while earning his fifth NBA championship — and a chance to win his fifth Finals MVP award — has eluded him since leading the Lakers to an NBA championship in 2019–20, James proved his championship mettle one more time during Team USA's run to gold at the 2024 Olympics in Paris.

"What a blessing to coach him finally after all these years of coaching against him and trying to figure out how to beat him," Team USA and Golden State Warriors head coach Steve Kerr said. "To watch him up close ... just to see his approach, to see his professionalism, how coachable he is. Then, of course, how gifted he is at everything, [how] every part of the game he seems to have mastered. I'm thrilled to have been able to coach him these last six weeks. I'm a LeBron fan for life."

In a career that has spanned a generation, James shows no signs of slowing down yet. However, when he does retire, in addition to all his records and achievements, he'll have one distinction that will likely go forever unchallenged: no one was greater for longer. ■

CAREER HIGHLIGHTS

- 4-time NBA Champion (2011–12, 2012–13, 2015–16, 2019–20)
- 4-time MVP (2008–09, 2009–10, 2011–12, 2012–13)
- 4-time Finals MVP (2011–12, 2012–13, 2015–16, 2019–20)
- 3-time All-Star Game MVP (2006, 2008, 2018)
- 21-time All Star

DENVER NUGGETS

15

Nikola JOKIC

POSITION C // **SHOOTS** RIGHT // **HEIGHT** 6'11" // **WEIGHT** 284 LBS // **DRAFTED** 2014, 41ST OVERALL

His nickname is perfect, because he makes the game fun.

Nikola Jokic, known as "The Joker," is the NBA's anti-star. He has no interest in the spotlight — his preferred offseason activity is being at home in his village of Sombor, Serbia, tending to his beloved horses.

When he's on the job he doesn't fly through the air or race past defenders in a blur. In a league full of sprinters, the Denver Nuggets star center shuffles. Despite standing nearly 7 feet tall, less than 2 percent of his field goal attempts have been dunks over the course of his career. By comparison, Giannis Antetokounmpo, the Milwaukee Bucks star who has been in the conversation with Jokic for league MVP honors so often, has scored more than 15 percent of his baskets by stuffing the ball through the rim with force.

Jokic has turned himself into an all-time great through a collection of feathery floaters, half-hooks and seeing-eye jumpers, all while using his other-worldly passing skills to keep defenses perpetually off-balance.

His style of play is unconventional — and explains why he was taken 41st overall in the 2014 draft — but also pleasing to the eye, as he uses his skill and his basketball intelligence to recognize and make plays ahead of everyone around him.

"He's playing the game, and you think he's not serious, but he's so effective," Hakeem Olajuwon, the Hall-of-Fame center for the Houston Rockets (who relied on no shortage of craftiness himself) said once as Jokic's star was ascending. "He doesn't look strong, but I see he gets such deep post position. I think maybe it's the mismatch, but then he does the same thing against bigger guys. His shot, his fakes, they are very difficult to time. You don't know when he's faking and when it's real. He has tricks!"

Most of the time Jokic looks like he's not trying and some of the time like he barely cares.

Famously, after leading the Nuggets to the 2023 NBA title, he admitted that mostly he was looking forward to everything being over after an extra-long playoff season.

"It's good. It's good," Jokic said after the Nuggets eliminated the Miami Heat in six games. "The job is done, and we can go home now."

Few have ever done the job better. At the end of 2023–24, Jokic collected his third MVP award in four seasons, the exception being the 2022–23 season, when he finished second in voting but got the ultimate consolation prize — the Finals MVP award after leading Denver to its first ever NBA title. He came in second in the voting again in 2024–25, joining Celtics greats Larry Bird and Bill Russell as the only players in league history to finish first or second in the voting for five-straight seasons.

Only the NBA's ultimate royalty can count three or more MVP awards and a Finals MVP award on their résumés. The list stops at eight, and all of those who have done it before Jokic are candidates for the league's Mount Rushmore: Kareem Abdul-Jabbar, Moses Malone, Michael Jordan, Wilt Chamberlain, Magic Johnson, Bird and LeBron James.

Since winning his first MVP award in 2020–21, Jokic has averaged 26.8 points, 12.3 rebounds, 9 assists and 1.4 steals per game while shooting 58.6 percent from the floor and 37.8 percent from three. The overall volume of his output combined with his offensive efficiency saw Jokic set a new bar for modern statistical measures. In 2020–21 Jokic led the NBA in metrics like PER (player efficiency rating), his production when adjusted for pace of play, and BPM (box plus minus), his production when his teammates' performances are factored in. In 2021–22 he set all-time records in both categories.

At times Jokic seems to toy with the game. In 2023–24 he had a stretch of 14 games when he shot 74 percent from the floor and 61.9 percent from three. In 2024–25 he had his best individual season yet. He became the first player in NBA history to finish top three in points per game (29.8, good for third), rebounds per game (12.7, also good for third) and assists per game (10.2, good for second) while connecting on 57.6 percent of his field goal attempts, including 41.7 percent from three. He also joined Oscar Robertson and Russell Westbrook as the only players to average a triple-double for a season.

Nikola Jokic drives to the basket against Isaiah Hartenstein of the Oklahoma City Thunder in Game 2 of the conference semifinals on May 7, 2025.

CAREER HIGHLIGHTS

- 2022–23 NBA Champion
- 3-time MVP (2020–21, 2021–22, 2023–24)
- 2022–23 Finals MVP
- 2022–23 Western Conference Finals MVP
- 7-time All Star

And even when the stakes get higher, his productivity never wavers. During the Nuggets' championship run, Jokic recorded triple-doubles in 10 of the Nuggets' 20 playoff games and logged some epic performances that further set him apart, such as a 53-point and 11-rebound showing in Game 4 versus the Phoenix Suns in the second round. He became the first player in Finals history to have a 30-20-10 triple-double, with 32 points, 21 rebounds and 10 assists in Game 3 at Miami.

"I know how great Jokic is," LeBron James said after the Nuggets eliminated the Lakers in the first round of the 2022–23 playoffs. "There are certain guys in this league that play the game a certain way, a certain way that I like to play the game as well, and he's one of them, where you are always off-balance when you are guarding a player like that because of his ability to score, rebound, shoot. He sees plays before they happen.

"There's not many guys in our league like that." ■

Jayson TATUM

POSITION SF, PF // **SHOOTS** RIGHT // **HEIGHT** 6'8" // **WEIGHT** 210 LBS // **DRAFTED** 2017, 3RD OVERALL

For Jayson Tatum, NBA stardom came quicky and easily.

He was drafted third overall out of Duke in 2017, and in less than a year found himself as the starting forward on a Boston Celtics team that won 55 games and went straight to the 2018 Eastern Conference Finals. Boston lost in seven to LeBron James and the Cleveland Cavaliers, but not before Tatum had announced himself as a star on the rise with a stellar postseason.

The 6-foot-8 wing averaged 18.5 points a game on 47.1 percent shooting over his first 19 playoff games and stepped it up when it mattered most, averaging 23 points on 49 percent shooting in the Celtics' three elimination games over their run.

Tatum's signature moment may have come in the fourth quarter of a tightly contested Game 7, when he drove left through the lane, rose up and posterized none other than James himself, instinctively flexing on the "King" on his way back up the floor.

"I meant no disrespect by it, just in the moment, made a play, just showing emotion," Tatum said.

But for all of Tatum's instant NBA success — he was an All Star and All-NBA player by his third season and has been a perennial name on the MVP voting ballot beginning in 2021–22 — the disappointments were mounting, too.

Jayson Tatum dribbles past Gary Trent Jr. of the Milwaukee Bucks in an October 28, 2024, game in Boston.

In 2019–20 the Celtics lost in the Eastern Conference Finals for the second time in Tatum's career, and in 2021–22 they lost in the Finals, falling in six games to the Golden State Warriors after leading the series 2-1. In 2022–23 they lost in the Eastern Conference Finals yet again, this time to the Miami Heat.

It's no wonder it was particularly sweet when Tatum and the Celtics finally broke through in 2023–24, capping a dominant 64-18 regular season with a 16-3 sprint through the

playoffs. At long last Tatum could get his hands on the trophy he'd been chasing from the moment he came into the NBA.

It only took everything.

"It took being relentless. It took being on the other side of this and losing in the Finals and being at literally the lowest point in a basketball career that you could be, to next year, to the following year, thinking that was going to be the time, and come up short again," said Tatum in the wake of the Celtics' win.

"And now, to elevate yourself in a space that, you know, all your favorite players are in, everybody that they consider greats or legends have won a championship, and all of the guys I looked up to won a championship, multiple championships.

"So now I can, like, walk in those rooms and be a part of that. It's a hell of a feeling. This is more — I dreamed about what it would be like, but this is 10 times better."

Perhaps what's most impressive about Tatum isn't his ability as a two-way star, capable of affecting games offensively and defensively, or that someone with his gifts can rise up and create highlight-reel plays while still being one of the most consistent and durable stars in the game. Since his rookie season he's ranked second in the NBA in minutes played in the regular season and leads the league in both games and minutes played in the postseason. Which made it all the more shocking when Tatum tore his Achilles tendon in the fourth game of Boston's second-round series against the New York Knicks in the 2025 playoffs — bringing Boston's title defense to a sudden end. The hope is that, given his age, he'll be able to make a full recovery and be ready for the 2026–27 season, if not sooner.

Regardless Tatum's level of accomplishment is impressive. Shortly after his injury he was named to the All-NBA First Team for the fourth-straight season. At 27, he already ranks fourth in all-time playoff scoring for Boston through just eight seasons and is Boston's all-time leader in points-per-game in the postseason — his nearly 23.8 per-game average puts him ahead of Boston legends like Larry Bird, John Havlicek and Paul Pierce, among other luminaries.

As the accolades accumulate — and health permitting — Tatum's status among Celtics and NBA greats will only continue to rise.

"I would love to be on the Mount Rushmore of Celtics. Bird, Russell, Paul Pierce and those guys," Tatum said in an interview with journalist Jeff Goodman prior to the start of the Celtics' championship season. "They paved the way. The one thing all those guys have is [championships]. I have to get to the top of the mountain to even be considered one of those guys. I want to be an all-time great, I want to be known as a winner, and I believe I will be." ■

CAREER HIGHLIGHTS

- > 2023–24 NBA Champion
- > 2021–22 Eastern Conference Finals MVP
- > 2023 All-Star Game MVP
- > 6-time All Star
- > 4-time All-NBA First Team

LEGENDS AMONG US

The Bay Area was the ideal location to take in the sun setting on three NBA legends. After all, for LeBron James, Kevin Durant and Stephen Curry, it was the site of many of their brightest moments, as they battled with and against each other for NBA supremacy for so many years.

Not that anyone is trying to rush them from the stage right now. Quite the contrary. Try to find anyone who wants to see three of this or any era's all-time greats step away from the spotlight. Or even try to make the argument that they should, given that they remain among the best players in the league well into their second or — in James' case — third decades.

The NBA's most accomplished active trio were in the middle of everything at the 2025 All-Star weekend in San Francisco. It wasn't a farewell but certainly an opportunity to reflect.

In basketball terms, the three are raging against the dying of the light more determinedly and effectively than almost anyone before them. In 2024–25, James was in his 22nd NBA season and playing better than any 40-year-old has ever played basketball. Durant was 36 and nearly as dominant in his 17th season as he was in almost any that came before. Curry turned 37 and was in his 16th year, and he was still the most dangerous three-point shooter in the game. But all good things — even nearly unprecedently great things — eventually come to an end. Exactly when that might be is a guess at best. All of them remain under contract. All of them remain elite. All of them remain committed to their craft. But time remains undefeated, and it's better to celebrate the league's most influential trio while we still can.

There are myriad ways to contextualize the significance of James and his peers' impact on the NBA, but first a little economics lesson: When James was playing basketball for St. Vincent–St. Mary High School in Akron, Ohio, the NBA was in a vastly different place than it is now. Not that the league was suffering. The Larry Bird–Magic Johnson era of the '80s and the Michael Jordan era of the '90s, combined with the stewardship of late NBA commissioner David Stern, had long ago placed the league on a growth curve it's still enjoying today. But it wasn't quite the fire-breathing money factory it seems to be now.

In 2002–03, the last year that the NBA didn't have LeBron James in it, the league was still adjusting to a post-Jordan future after the Bulls star had retired (for the second time) in 1998–99. Even Jordan's brief comeback with the Washington Wizards didn't help. Television ratings were off from their peak, the Lakers' Shaquille O'Neal–Kobe Bryant mini-dynasty was splintering and the game was at times tough to watch. When the San Antonio Spurs won the 2003 title over the New Jersey Nets, the average score was 88–82 for the six-game series. The Spurs scored 101 points in Game 1 and didn't crack 100 again, and the Nets never did, even with Hall-of-Fame point guard Jason Kidd pushing the pace. In Game 4 the final score was 77–76.

Those aren't the only reasons the financial picture was so much more different then, but it all played a part. In the last season before James was drafted in the summer of 2003, the NBA salary cap was $40.27 million. That's it. That's the pool from which an entire NBA roster was to be paid (unless teams went over the cap and paid the luxury tax). In other words, an entire team could conceivably earn less than the $40.5 million Sacramento Kings center Domantas Sabonis earned just for the 2024–25 season. In 2024–25 the salary cap was $140.6 million. Adjusted for inflation, that $40.27 million is around $69 million today, meaning that in real dollars NBA player salaries have more than doubled in the span of James' career. And the

LeBron James is congratulated by commissioner David Stern at the 2003 NBA Draft. In the 20-plus years since James went first overall to the Cleveland Cavaliers, the landscape of the NBA has changed significantly, in large part thanks to James and his immense influence.

best is yet to come if you're in the business of being an NBA superstar.

Let's say Durant plays until his 22nd season, which would be in 2030–31. Sure, it seems unlikely, but so is putting up 26.6 points, 6 rebounds and 4.2 assists with a True Shooting percentage (TS%) of 64.2 (which is better than his preposterous career average of 62 percent) as Durant did in season 17. If he keeps it rolling until 2030–31, when he'll be 41, the NBA salary cap is projected to be $200.6 million, or more than a five-fold increase since the LeBron era kicked off. That type of growth will be made possible by the league's new media rights deal, which kicks in in 2025–26 and will pay the NBA $76 billion over the next 11 seasons. There are a lot of big-picture reasons why media companies want to invest that much money in the NBA, especially in a time when the means of delivering content seems to be shifting by the minute. But perhaps the overwhelming reason is that the NBA delivers star power to a global audience as reliably as movie franchises based on comic book characters do, and going on two full decades now, James, Durant and Curry have been the league's most beloved superheroes.

"Guys in this league owe a great deal to these guys," said Garrett Temple, the Toronto Raptors wing and longtime member of the National Basketball Players Association (NBPA) executive who has carved out a 15-year career as a respected journeyman. "They helped the game go global, because of what they've been able to do. Obviously, a lot of credit goes to the late David Stern, to NBA commissioner Adam Silver and them promoting it globally. But what these stars have been able to do is carry themselves well and show a tremendous passion for basketball, and so people all over the world fall in love with them. At the end of the day, they've left the game in a better place."

Of course, they're still in the game. And while the 2025 All-Star weekend was decidedly less about competition and more about pomp and circumstance, perhaps the most amazing quality of the James-Durant-Curry trio is that they can still absolutely bring it. Each of them brought it during the 2024–25 season and all three were at the All-Star Game entirely on merit. I referenced Durant's 2024–25 numbers earlier, but James arrived in San Francisco averaging 24.3 points, 7.7 rebounds and 9 assists with an effective field goal percentage (eFG%) of 57.8, a better mark than he had in three of his four MVP seasons. Curry was holding up his end, too. Even in a down year on an injury-riddled team with little in the way of offensive help (until the Warriors added Jimmy Butler, another bag of bones who can still do it age 35), Curry was averaging 23.4 points, 6.1 assists and 4.5 rebounds before the All-Star weekend. By the end of the season, Curry had

made over 300 threes in a season (311 to be exact) for the sixth time. For context, only four other players have ever made 300-plus triples in a single season — James Harden, Klay Thompson, Anthony Edwards and Malik Beasley — and none of them have done it more than once.

And in case the world needed a reminder of what the old guys can do when the stakes are highest, the 2024 Olympic tournament in Paris was the "forever moment" for their shared dominance. Over two epic medal-round games, which encompassed a razor-thin semifinal win by Team USA over Serbia and another hard-fought win against the home team, France, for gold, the best basketball in the world was being played by the three guys whose NBA Draft dates almost pre-date the iPhone. That it happened in what is likely the most competitive international tournament ever — Serbia (with Nikola Jokic), Greece (with Giannis Antetokounmpo), Canada (with Shai Gilgeous-Alexander) and France (with Victor Wembanyama) were all anchored by past and, likely, future NBA MVPs — is even more fitting.

"I hope that the legacy of this team is to see these superstar players and the emotion and how much it matters to [them] to win," said Team USA head coach Steve Kerr to a small group of reporters after the gold-medal game. "And then hopefully the stories will be out there of how hard Kevin Durant works every day, and ... LeBron and Steph and all these guys. And that's the key. We've got a lot of talent in this country that all the young players watching this need to know how hard it is to win, how much goes into it."

Let's start there. The NBA's three biggest stars are each almost weirdly gifted. There's no denying that. This is not exactly a story of underdogs overcoming impossible adversity with their grit alone. The NBA doesn't work that way. Supreme talent is the

^ Kevin Durant, Victor Wembanyama and LeBron James play in the men's gold-medal game between France and the United States during the Paris 2024 Olympics. Team USA won against the host France 98–87.

entry fee. Even now, more than two decades after James averaged 20.9 points, 5.5 rebounds and 5.9 assists as a 19-year-old straight out of high school, watching him around other NBA players is a little mind bending. He remains enormous for a forward and looks comfortable against most of the league's centers, all while moving like a shooting guard who's 15 years younger. And even with all the advantages you get with being 6-foot-9 and 260 pounds (he's listed at 250 pounds, but no one believes that) James has famously invested in his health and physical fitness to an unprecedented degree. There are numbers that get floated around. Back in 2016 Bill Simmons of *The Ringer* said that Maverick Carter, James' longtime business partner, told him (Simmons) that James spent $1.5 million on his body, splashing out on everything from personal chefs to NBA-level workout facilities in his homes to cryotherapy chambers, multiple personal trainers and other treatment professionals. It's possible that number has doubled now. The investment has more than paid off, given that James became the first active NBA player to become a billionaire, as calculated by Forbes, back in 2022.

And what of Durant? He's listed at 6-foot-11 but may actually be 7 feet tall. And ever since he was drafted No. 2 overall in 2007 after one season at the University of Texas, he's been some version of what he is now: a silky shooter and a brilliant ball handler, the combination of which no one had seen in the NBA at his size before he arrived. And he continued to get better. In 2009–10 Durant led the NBA in scoring — the first of four times he's done it — and shot 50.6 percent from two-point range and 36.5 percent from three with a TS% of 60.7. In any context it was an impressive display of efficiency for a high-volume scorer, particularly for a 21-year-old in his third season. But jump ahead a decade and consider these numbers from Durant's age 32 to age 35 seasons: even though injuries limited him to just 212 games over four seasons, somehow Durant has been a better and more efficient scorer at the later stage of his career than he was when he was runner-up for MVP and winning his first scoring

Kevin Durant drives past Donovan Mitchell of the Cleveland Cavaliers in a game on March 21, 2025. In his 17th season, he averaged 26.6 points and 6 rebounds.

LeBron James celebrates breaking Kareem Abdul-Jabbar's scoring record on February 7, 2023.

title with the Oklahoma City Thunder. It's kind of astounding. In his early 30s and battling injuries every season, playing on different teams with a shifting cast of running mates, Durant averaged 28.2 points a game while shooting 58 percent on twos and 40.9 percent on threes with a TS% of 64.6.

And then there's Curry. It's easy to make him the plucky one because he's relatively average by way of height at 6-foot-3, but he's miles from the skinny kid at Davidson who lit up March Madness every year. Curry has always been an athletic savant. Just pull up some of his golf videos or watch him sink trick shots from the tunnel as part of his warm-up routine to recognize that. But to see Curry up close at age 37 is to see an athlete who has sculpted himself, carefully adding layers of muscle over time. The ankle problems that threatened his career over his first three professional seasons were solved with surgery and a diligent rehabilitation process that Curry maintains to this day. In 2011–12 Curry was limited to just 27 games. But he used that time to attack and solve the problem, and from 2012–13 to 2016–17 Curry was an All-NBA selection four times, an MVP twice and an NBA champion twice, and he took part in three Finals while playing in 96 percent of 491 regular season and playoff games. At the same time he was developing himself into the greatest shooter that's ever played the sport. There are only four players in NBA history to make at least 1,000 threes and shoot better than 42 percent for their careers, and none have done it while shooting more than 5 threes per game. Curry has done it while shooting more than 9 threes per game. He has averaged nearly 4 made threes per game for his career — the next closest is Damian Lillard, with 3.1. No one shoots it like Curry, but his prowess has inspired a new way to play the game and a new generation of players who have shaped their talents in Curry's mold.

"The game has changed based on those three guys," said Houston Rockets forward Jeff Green, who broke into the NBA with Durant in 2007 and went to the 2018 Finals with James and the Cleveland Cavs, losing to Durant and Curry with the Warriors. "Steph being the best shooter of all time, and the other two guys being — LeBron's what? 6-8, 6-9, and whatever KD wants to be, but 7-foot — able to do everything possible on the court, having the IQ that all three have, they all revolutionized the game: how you have to play it, the way you work at it, the longevity, the professionalism. Every one of those three guys are all of that ... I mean, that's years and years and years of hard work ... you don't get to become the NBA's best shooter of all-time by mistake. You don't play as long as LeBron and KD have by accident. You know the hard work that they've put in. You see it. And you know that's why they are who they are."

Accordingly, the milestones and honors have piled up. Between them they share 10 NBA titles, seven Finals MVP awards, seven regular-season MVPs, 19 Finals appearances, 47 All-Star Games and nine Olympic gold medals. They keep setting the bar at new and seemingly impossible heights. Consider these points:

> Already the all-time scoring leader, if James continues to score in 2025–26 — his last under contract, though no one is expecting him to retire any time soon — at the rate he has the previous two seasons, James could eclipse 44,000 points. That would leave him nearly 5,000 points ahead of Kareem Abdul-Jabbar, whose once seemingly unbreakable record James surpassed in 2023–24. Just for fun, let's presume James stops there and packs it in while still near the peak of his powers. In that scenario Kevin Durant — who became just the eighth player in NBA history to score 30,000 points in February 2025 — would have to play at least seven more seasons to catch James, and that assumes Durant averages 27 points a game and plays 62 games or more each of those seasons, which he did in 2024–25 but has done only one other time in the past seven seasons. Or how about 26-year-old Luka Doncic? The Slovenian star, who led the NBA in scoring in 2023–24, would have to average more than 28 points a game and play at least 67 games a season until 2041–42, when he would be turning 43, or three years older than James is now.

> Here's the thing about Durant: He's second in active scoring (to James) and eighth all-time even while having had four seasons where he's played less than 50 games due to injuries, including missing all of the 2019–20 season. He's the only player in NBA history to average 27 points a game for his career with a TS% of 62 or better. No wonder his peers consider him the most lethal scorer to have ever played: "It's a combination of being a three-level scorer and the efficiency that he has had his whole career. I know we're both kind of obsessed with the 50/40/90 pursuit — and he got it one year [in Golden State]," Curry told ESPN as Durant was closing in on 30,000 points. "But the way he does it is totally different than the way I do it. Just the fact that he's such a graceful, efficient scorer no matter what defense you really throw at him, to do it for that many years is really impressive. So there's a reason people talk about him as the greatest legitimate scorer ever."

Stephen Curry celebrates after scoring his record-breaking 2,974th three-pointer during a game against the New York Knicks on December 14, 2021.

> And Curry? If he plays three more seasons after 2024–25 at his current level of production, he'll crack 30,000 points as well, joining Durant and James among the top 10 leading scorers of all-time. But it's his three-point shooting milestones where Curry may forever stand alone. Every three-pointer he makes pushes his NBA record for career threes even further out of reach. If the Warriors sharpshooter makes 250 threes a season for the next three years — he made 311 in 2024–25 — he'll top 4,800 triples. James Harden, his closest active pursuer, would need to make nearly 200 threes a season — or just above his career average of 196 a year — for 12 more seasons, which seems unlikely given the Clippers guard is 35 and just finished his 16th year. Trae Young is one of the most prolific of a generation of guards who have styled their games after Curry, but he's only averaged 182.4 made threes through his first seven seasons. At that pace he'd have to play 27 years to catch Curry if he wants to get to 4,800. Or how about single-season excellence? Curry is the only player in NBA history to make 400 threes in a season; he made 402 in 2015–16, his second MVP season. The next best single-season total belongs to Harden, who had 378 in 2018–19 but has never again cracked 300. In 2024–25 Anthony Edwards put together one of the greatest non-Curry three-point seasons ever, his 320 made threes the seventh-best single season total ever, and the most by anyone other than Curry or Harden. But Curry's 402 threes came about when he shot 45.4 percent on more than 11 attempts a game in a season in which he played 79 games. So while Edwards assembled an incredible season, he was he still 82 threes short of tying Curry's mark. Edwards is just 23 so you can't rule out that he'll take a run at Curry's single-season mark again, but he'll have to average more than one more made three per game — assuming he plays all 82 games — to somehow pull ahead of Curry's single-season best.

The "too long, didn't read" version: James, Durant and Curry each have a list of individual and team accomplishments that won't be replicated soon, if ever.

So what happens when they inevitably step aside? It's the NBA's multibillion-dollar question. The league's solution to breaking out of the post-Jordan doldrums in the early 2000s was to embrace rule changes that opened up the game and set the course for the "space-and-pace" era that has driven scoring and offensive efficiency to new heights. Since James' rookie season the league's average points per 100 possessions has increased from 102.9, the lowest of the three-point era, to 115.3 in 2023–24, an all-time high — as was the 26.9 assists per game teams averaged. There are questions about whether the league's embrace of the three-point shot has gone too far, with teams averaging a record 37.6 triples per game in 2024–25, a 40.4 percent increase compared to the 22.4 threes per game teams were averaging a decade ago, when Curry won his first title. The NBA is also embracing international basketball like never before, as it aggressively looks into creating a league in Europe under the NBA brand after making significant investments in Africa. Aligning itself with global titans like Amazon for its latest media rights deal can't hurt.

But chances are the NBA will secure its post–James-Durant-Curry future the same way it elevated itself once Jordan retired: new generations of stars will come along doing things that seemed unfathomable until they were done. Spurs big man Victor Wembanyama is showing signs that he can reshape the game with his prodigious gifts. Three-time MVP Nikola Jokic is putting together a statistical résumé that will be unique across basketball as he melds the perimeter skills of an elite point guard with a dominant paint presence. Shai Gilgeous-Alexander is posting season averages last achieved by Michael Jordan, and Anthony Edwards has drawn his share of Jordan comparisons, too, for his ferocious athleticism, while shooting better than Jordan ever did from the three-point line. Luka Doncic made the All-NBA First Team five-straight seasons before turning 26, something even James didn't do. There are other candidates.

"The league is in a different place now [than in the post-Jordan era]," said New Orleans Pelicans guard CJ McCollum, a 12-year veteran and another member of the NBPA executive. "And obviously you've got a lot of young stars. Giannis [Antetokounmpo] is still only 30, right? There's Jayson Tatum, Luka, ANT [Anthony Edwards], Ja [Morant], Wemby, Shai. There's a lot of players who are — obviously not at that level — but they have a potential to be faces of the league, stars, win multiple championships, win multiple MVPs, be global figures. I think we're in a really good place, but I think we have to just appreciate LeBron, KD and Steph while they're here." ■

GAME CHANGERS

Donovan Mitchell

10 Jimmy BUTLER

POSITION SF, SG, PF // **SHOOTS** RIGHT // **HEIGHT** 6'7" // **WEIGHT** 230 LBS // **DRAFTED** 2011, 30TH OVERALL

For all the aggravation the Jimmy Butler experience can bring to a franchise, it's worth it.

That's the only conclusion to be drawn after the mercurial superstar breaks up with a team, often in contentious fashion, only to find another team waiting with open arms, in large part because he delivers the goods.

Butler may not have the stats or the celebrity cachet of some of the NBA's biggest stars, but when it comes to winning basketball games in the most competitive environments, few are better.

It's why the Golden State Warriors, determined to extend the championship window of then-37-year-old franchise legend Stephen Curry, decided to trade for Butler in February 2025 even though he had been suspended by the Miami Heat three times in the space of a month — once for "conduct detrimental to the team," another for missing a team flight and another for walking out of practice — as he tried to get the team to trade him after six seasons in southern Florida.

It's why the Heat were eager to acquire Butler even after he had a falling out with then-Philadelphia 76ers head coach Brett Brown during the 2018–19 season, and why the Sixers traded for Butler after he publicly demanded to be dealt from Minnesota prior to the start of that same season, and why Minnesota had acquired Butler from Chicago after he asked to be traded from the Bulls following the 2016–17 season.

In each case the team that Butler leaves gets worse, and the team that he joins gets better, at least until the rugged 6-foot-7 wing gets frustrated with his teammates or coaches, expresses his frustrations publicly and starts the cycle again.

But there is no questioning Butler's ability to lift teams. As a six-time All Star who has been an All-NBA selection five times and an All-Defensive choice five times, he's one of the most well-rounded players in the league — one whose intelligence, playmaking and ability to draw fouls and defend even the most talented players translate so perfectly to the postseason.

"It's been amazing. He's of the best players in the league. He's instantly transformed our team," Warriors coach Steve Kerr said after Butler arrived at the 2024–25 trade deadline and breathed new life into the Warriors' title hopes in the latter stages of Curry's career. "We're 16-4 since we got him. He's a very unique talent. He's a superstar, but he's a subtle superstar. He doesn't wow you with his leaping ability or shooting prowess or speed. It's just his brute strength and his brain. He is one of the smartest players I've ever been around, and his ability to just generate open shot after open shot is impressive, and he's obviously a great two-way player. He's a hell of a defender. We're lucky to have him."

Butler's rise is part of his legend. He grew up in tough circumstances just outside of Houston, Texas. His father left the family when he was an infant, and his mother — according to Butler — kicked him out of the house when he was 13. He lived with friends' families through high school and, while a good player, was unrecruited out of high school and had to attend junior college to keep playing. He was offered a scholarship at Marquette University and was part of successful teams all three years there, but he never earned individual recognition other than All-Conference honorable mentions for his junior and senior seasons. Butler was the 30th overall pick by the Chicago Bulls in 2011, and he played only limited minutes as a rookie and didn't start until his third season. He had to fight for stardom, finally gaining recognition as an All Star in his fourth season.

Butler's physical, two-way play became his trademark.

From 2018–19 to 2024–25 Butler was one of four players to start at least 80 playoff games, but the only one to play for three different teams while doing it, as he helped the Sixers and the Warriors to second-round showings and the Miami Heat to two Finals appearances. During this stretch, he logged 23.3 points, 6.5 rebounds, 5.5 assists and 1.7 steals playing against the NBA's best in the most heated environments.

"Everybody remembers winning, that's it. They don't care how many points you score, they only care if you won or lost," Butler said during the 2020 Finals, where the Heat lost to the Los Angeles Lakers in six games.

Jimmy Butler slam dunks the ball in Game 1 of the Golden State Warriors' first-round series against the Houston Rockets on April 20, 2025.

The Heat were down 2-0 in the series and effectively facing elimination when Butler put them on his back, notching 40 points, 11 rebounds, 13 assists, 2 steals and 2 blocks while leading Miami to a much-needed Game 3 win.

"Look, how do you — how else do you say it other than Jimmy effing Butler?" Heat head coach Erik Spoelstra said later. "... It's really hard to analyze or describe Jimmy until you actually feel him between the four lines. He's a supreme, elite competitor and we needed it.

"Obviously this was a very desperate urgent game, and he was doing it on both ends of the court, just put his imprint on every important part of the game."

Butler did it again when the Heat were facing elimination in Game 5, as he posted his second Finals triple-double — 35 points, 11 rebounds, 12 assists and 5 steals while playing 47 minutes, most of them guarding the Lakers' LeBron James.

When Butler led the Heat to the Finals in 2023 as the eighth seed, he averaged 37.6 points per game as the Heat upset the No. 1–seed Milwaukee Bucks in six games in the first round.

"His will to win is remarkable," said Spoelstra. "... every young player coming into this league should study footage on Jimmy Butler, the definition of a two-way player competing on both ends."

CAREER HIGHLIGHTS

- 2022–23 Eastern Conference MVP
- 2014–15 Most Improved Player
- 6-time All Star
- 2022–23 All-NBA Second Team
- 5-time All-Defensive Second Team

5 Anthony EDWARDS

POSITION SG // **SHOOTS** RIGHT // **HEIGHT** 6'4" // **WEIGHT** 225 LBS // **DRAFTED** 2020, 1ST OVERALL

It almost isn't fair.

Anthony Edwards was already an opponent's nightmare. He stands 6-foot-4 and carries a thick build that wouldn't look out of place in the NFL — in fact, as a youngster growing up in Georgia, he was recognized first as a budding football prospect before he ever took up basketball.

He can move that body like his joints are lubricated with grease, and he's got the ball-handling skills to match. He can slither around screens or cross over the NBA's best defenders, leaving only a vapor trail for them to wave at. That's if he doesn't plow right through them.

And if he gets half a step? Look out.

In his first four seasons with the Minnesota Timberwolves, Edwards very quickly became the most feared dunker in the NBA. His speed, agility and ball-handling ability combined with his extraordinary explosiveness made him a menace to whomever dared challenge him at the rim.

There were "poster dunks" from so many games, perhaps none more famous than when he climbed the ladder to dunk on Utah Jazz forward John Collins during the third quarter of a March 2024 game that sent a charge through the Delta Center, Collins to the dressing room with a bruise to his forehead and social media into a frenzy. It also sparked the Timberwolves to a comeback win.

Anthony Edwards dunks over Kevon Looney of the Golden State Warriors in Game 3 of the second round of the playoffs on May 10, 2025.

"The things he can do, above the rim, below the rim, his strength as a basketball player, when you see him jump like that, a lot of people don't continue to go higher. They don't continue to go forward. They get bumped and they kind of [get] pushed back," T-wolves veteran guard Mike Conley told reporters afterward. "He's like a cat almost; he keeps going forward, lands on his feet.

"Stuff like that is what makes him who he is and why he can maneuver in the game how he does."

But if there was one small gap in Edwards' tool kit — and to be clear, Edwards' choice of tools is so overflowing that he already had two All-Star nods and an All-NBA Second Team honor by the end of the 2023–24 season — it was that he was only an average shooter by NBA standards.

Through his first three years he was shooting just 35.3 percent from behind the three-point line. Not terrible, but it was something opposing defenses could surrender to him as they packed the lane to make his attacks on the rim more difficult.

But by season five, Edwards had had enough of that and did something about it. By the end of the 2024–25 season, one of the most explosive and athletic players of his (or any other) era also became one of the NBA's best-ever three-point shooters.

As I said, it's almost unfair.

During his fifth season Edwards launched a career-high 811 threes and converted them at a career-best 39.5 percent. The result was one of the most prolific shooting seasons in NBA history as Edwards' 320 made threes not only led the NBA but were the seventh-highest single-season total of all time, behind Stephen Curry's five-best shooting seasons and the best shooting season of James Harden's career.

It also made Edwards one of only five players in league history — Curry did it six times, Harden, Klay Thompson and Malik Beasley did it once each — to make at least 300 triples in a season.

From high-flying dunker to elite three-point threat?

It seems almost impossible, but that's Edwards: a player whose talent defies category, almost.

Did I mention that in the summer of 2024 he played on Team USA at the Olympics in Paris, where, as the youngest member of a gold-medal winning squad, he got the opportunity to soak up firsthand lessons from the likes of LeBron James, Kevin Durant and Curry?

Since coming into the NBA as the No. 1 pick out of Georgia, Edwards has established himself as a potentially all-time talent.

Over his career so far, he's averaged 23.9 points, 5.3 rebounds, 4.2 assists and 1.3 steals. The only other players to average at least 23 points, 5 rebounds, 4 assists and 1 steal with at least 250 games played are Kareem Abdul-Jabbar, Michael Jordan, James and Luka Doncic — three of the very best players in NBA history and Doncic, who was named to the All-NBA First Team four times in his first five seasons. And among that group none were anywhere close to Edwards' 1,109 made threes in his first five seasons.

The best may yet be still to come: In 2024–25 Edwards averaged a career-best 27.6 points per game along with 5.7 rebounds, 4.5 assists and 1.2 assists. Along the way he joined James, Jordan, Doncic and Hall of Famer Tracy McGrady as the only players to have accumulated at least 2,100 points, 450 rebounds, 350 assists and 90 steals in a single season before turning 24.

And he did it all while leading the Minnesota Timberwolves to the playoffs for the fourth consecutive season — the longest stretch for the franchise since 2003–04 — and to the conference finals twice, which is a franchise first.

But that taste of success has only made him more determined to go that step further.

"I'm going to work my butt off this summer," Edwards said after Minnesota lost in five games to the Oklahoma City Thunder in the 2025 Western Conference Finals. "Nobody's going to work harder than me this summer. I'll tell you that much."

That might be unfair for the rest of the NBA. ■

CAREER HIGHLIGHTS

- > 3-time All Star
- > 2-time All-NBA Second Team
- > 2020–21 All-Rookie First Team

De'Aaron FOX

POSITION PG // **SHOOTS** LEFT // **HEIGHT** 6'3" // **WEIGHT** 185 LBS // **DRAFTED** 2017, 5TH OVERALL

Someone had to do it.

Someone had to look at the San Antonio Spurs and the opportunity of teaming with Victor Wembanyama, a generational talent barely scratching the surface of his potential, and decide, "yup, that's where I want to be for the prime of my career."

De'Aaron Fox did exactly that. Midway through his seventh season, the All-Star point guard left the Sacramento Kings — the team that drafted him fifth overall out of Kentucky and the place where he helped lift one of the NBA's traditionally wayward franchises back to respectability and the playoffs in 2022–23. He let the powers know that he didn't intend to sign a long-term contract extension and that his preferred trade destination was San Antonio.

That set in motion the February 3, 2025, deal that landed the then-27-year-old Fox in San Antonio, with the idea that he could spend his prime helping the 21-year-old French star break through as part of an up-and-coming playoff contender.

"I just felt this could be a special team," said Fox after the trade. "Not many guys come around like that. And, I think, not just him but everybody else [in the Spurs' young core]. I felt like the fit would be spectacular. And I feel like I have a lot of years left to play."

It didn't take long after the deal went down for Fox to show why the Spurs thought he would be the right fit with what they're trying to build.

In his Spurs debut, Fox scored 24 points and added 13 assists, as Wembanyama's go-ahead free throw with 2.4 seconds remaining gave the Spurs a thrilling 126–125 victory over the Atlanta Hawks.

"[Wembanyama] is different," Fox said. "He is special. Just the type of defensive attention he receives allows you to do things you don't normally do."

And from Wembanyama's point of view? "It's a surprise for nobody," he said. "We're all for it. We all enjoy it. It puts a lot on the table for us."

What Fox should bring to the table is the chance for the Spurs to do things they haven't normally done. It's not just that the lightning-quick guard has a long track record of being able to create offense for himself and for others. Over his last three full seasons in Sacramento, Fox was one of just four guards (Luka Doncic, Trae Young and Damian Lillard were the others) to average at least 25 points and 6 assists per game. Adding to that, Fox

was the only guard to put up 25 and 6 while averaging at least 1.5 steals — living up to his "Swipa" nickname.

Fox has shown himself to be one of the most dangerous late-game threats in the league, as demonstrated in 2022–23, when he led the NBA in points scored in the last five minutes of games in which the score is within five points or less. For his efforts that season, he won the inaugural Jerry West Trophy for Clutch Player of the Year.

"You can't be afraid to fail," Fox said on the TNT broadcast of the announcement. "Obviously, you're not going to make every shot, but my teammates, my coaches, they put me in position to succeed. So the least I can do is have confidence in myself to take good shots."

But Fox is dangerous at all points of the game. His first weapon is his speed. There are few if any guards in the NBA who get from one end to another as rapidly as Fox does. It keeps defenses on their heels and creates easy scoring opportunities against opponents who don't have their transition defense completely sewn up.

"I think if you look at [the Spurs'] pace, it has gone up," Brooklyn Nets head coach Jordi Fernandez (formerly an assistant coach in Sacramento) said shortly after the trade. "And De'Aaron is a one-man fast break. What dictates the pace is usually the point guard. He is, I think, the fastest in the world."

And he's deadly in half-court settings as well.

At the time of the trade Fox ranked 17th in the NBA in field goal attempts out of the pick-and-roll, but even with that volume he was the most efficient scorer as a pick-and-roll ball handler, with an effective field goal percentage of 57.8. Meanwhile the Spurs ranked 28th in the league in possessions finished by the pick-and-roll ball handler and 25th in points per possession in that setting, according to Synergy Sports. The addition of a dynamic scoring guard like Fox should only help unlock the Spurs offense.

De'Aaron Fox rises up against Oklahoma City Thunder center Isaiah Hartenstein in a game on March 2, 2025, in San Antonio.

CAREER HIGHLIGHTS

- 2022–23 Clutch Player of the Year
- 2023 All Star
- 2022–23 All-NBA Third Team

Fox's magic move is his floater — a shot he can get to with ease as teams must respect his speed and quickness and tend to retreat to the rim when he attacks out of a pick-and-roll.

It doesn't take much imagination to see defenses struggling to defend Fox off the dribble and simultaneously monitor the threat of Wembanyama — he of the nearly 10-foot standing reach — finishing lob passes as the roll man.

"It sure brings an interesting perspective," Wembanyama said. "I think that our goals for this season are even more attainable. We've got to use all of our strengths. We just added a big [one]."

It was disappointing, then, that Fox and Wembanyama only got to play five games together before the Spurs big man had to miss the rest of the 2024–25 season due to a blood clot in his shoulder.

But the Spurs made the move for Fox with an eye on the future rather than the present, and with Fox in the fold, the future looks bright. ■

Tyrese HALIBURTON

POSITION PG, SG // **SHOOTS** RIGHT // **HEIGHT** 6'5" // **WEIGHT** 185 LBS // **DRAFTED** 2020, 12TH OVERALL

Being one of the best players in the NBA isn't easy.

Now, some players make it look that way. LeBron James' metronomic excellence over two decades or Nikola Jokic's seemingly endless stacking of peak seasons or Giannis Antetokounmpo's tireless impersonation of a human wrecking ball would be the most obvious exceptions to the notion that being among the best 10 or 15 players on Earth is an exceedingly difficult thing to do.

But, by definition, it is hard. Injuries, inconsistencies, the intensity of the competition all make getting to the top of the NBA pyramid — let alone staying there — an ongoing struggle.

Few know this better than Tyrese Haliburton, who enjoyed a steady rise to the games' highest reaches and then faced a slew of challenges just when he got there.

First things first: the Indiana Pacers guard exceeded all but perhaps his own expectations when he earned All-NBA Third Team recognition following the 2023–24 season. But within that season was a novel.

For the first three months of 2023–24, Haliburton played point guard as well as almost any player ever has. It was like he broke the code, as he averaged 24.8 points and 12.8 assists on 63.9 percent True Shooting, knocking down 41 percent of his threes on nearly nine attempts a game.

For context, the only player in league history to even average 22 and 12 over a full season was Magic Johnson, who did it twice — in 1986–87 and 1988–89 — but his peak True Shooting was 62.5 percent.

Given the trajectory Haliburton was on — coming off his first All-Star season in 2022–23 in which he averaged 20.1 points and 10.4 assists and shot 40 percent from three for a True Shooting percentage of 62.4, a quartet of statistical thresholds never before achieved — it looked like he had arrived as an NBA great. Given he was just 22 when he did it, it seemed to indicate something legendary was about to unfold. It peaked when Haliburton led the Pacers to the Finals of the inaugural NBA Cup.

"People have said MVP, or All-NBA All Star or whatever," Haliburton said. "But at the end of the day I just want to play basketball, and I want to succeed as a team. I know [with] the team's success, individual success comes with that.

"So I think that that's been something that I really enjoyed about our run right now, is that it's forced the media to talk about what's in front of them, which is basketball. And I think as a person who loves the sport, I think everybody can appreciate that."

It was all heady stuff for a kid from Oshkosh, Wisconsin, who was a three-star recruit coming out of high school, turned himself into the 12th overall pick in the 2020 draft out of Iowa State and was traded from Sacramento to Indiana midway through his second season.

But the NBA can challenge even the best when they're at their peak. Just as Haliburton was playing at nearly unprecedented levels and the Pacers' blindingly fast attack was turning the league upside down, he injured his hamstring in January 2024. Even after he returned, his play suffered: he averaged just 16.8 points, 9.3 assists on 45.3 shooting, including 32.4 percent from three. He was only marginally better during the Pacers' surprise run to the Eastern Conference Finals, and after reaggravating his hamstring in the summer, he was essentially a spectator on the U.S. Olympic team as the Americans won gold in Paris.

His struggles continued early in 2024–25, and the Pacers struggled early too as they started the season 10-15, but Haliburton regained his form and the Pacers took off. He averaged 19.2 points and 9.6 assists with a True Shooting percentage of 64.7 from mid-December on, and Indiana went 40-17 after their slow start. Haliburton earned All-NBA Third Team honors again, and the Pacers emerged as a rising force in the Eastern Conference, advancing to the NBA Finals for the first time since 1999–2000 before falling in seven games to the Oklahoma City Thunder. But even when he was at his best, bad fortune lingered just around the corner, as he tore his Achilles tendon in the first quarter of Game 7. It meant that Haliburton wasn't able to deliver one more signature moment in a postseason run that was full of them: he counted four game-winning or game-tying baskets in the final five seconds of the fourth quarter and overtime during the Pacers' run — the record for a single postseason.

"He's a baller and a hooper and really just a gamer," said his then-teammate Myles Turner after Haliburton's buzzer-beating jumper helped the Pacers upset the Thunder in Game 1 of the Finals. "When it comes to the moments, he wants the ball. He wants to be the one to hit that shot. He doesn't shy away from the moment, and it's very important this time of the year to have a go-to guy. He just keeps finding a way."

Tyrese Haliburton shoots a three-pointer against the Chicago Bulls on December 6, 2024, in Chicago.

CAREER HIGHLIGHTS

- 2-time All Star
- 2 time All-NBA Third Team
- 2020–21 All-Rookie First Team

Kawhi LEONARD

POSITION SF // **SHOOTS** RIGHT // **HEIGHT** 6'7" // **WEIGHT** 225 LBS // **DRAFTED** 2011, 15TH OVERALL

For a player of Kawhi Leonard's talent and accomplishment, his stated goals are remarkably — and tellingly — modest.

"Just be able to be healthy, that's my No. 1 goal," Leonard said at the introductory press conference with the Toronto Raptors on the eve of training camp for the 2018–19 season.

He added, "Play a long, healthy career [and] be able to be dominant, wherever I land."

This wasn't LeBron James and the "Heat-les" — Dwyane Wade and Chris Bosh — being feted like rock stars and speculating the number of championships they would win in the summer of 2010.

This was a then-25-year-old who had already come face-to-face with his NBA mortality, having missed all but nine games of the 2017–18 season due to problems with his right leg. His injuries were part of what precipitated his team, the San Antonio Spurs, to trade him to the Toronto Raptors in the summer of 2018.

By that point Leonard had evolved from a defense-first prospect taken 15th overall in 2011 to the best two-way player in the sport and a means for the Spurs to extend their championship window with veterans Tim Duncan, Manu Ginobili and Tony Parker.

Leonard established himself fully in the 2014 Finals against the Miami Heat when — with the series tied 1-1 — Leonard turned into a force of nature. Over the last three games of the series, he averaged 23.7 points and 9.3 rebounds per game while shooting 68 percent from the floor and 53.8 percent from three, chipping in 2 steals and 2 blocks as he lifted the Spurs to the last title of the "Tim-Manu-Tony" era and earning Finals MVP honors in the process.

"Kawhi's a really quiet young man. But he listens and he's a great learner and super competitive," said then-Spurs head coach Gregg Popovich after the series. "[He] has a drive to be the best ..."

Leonard's star kept rising. He earned recognition as the NBA's Defensive Player of the Year in 2014–15, and when Duncan took a step back in 2015–16 and then retired before the following season, Leonard put together two of the best two-way seasons of the modern era — averaging 23.4 points, 3.1 assists, 6.3 rebounds and 1.8 steals with a True Shooting percentage of 61.3 from

CAREER HIGHLIGHTS

- 2-time NBA Champion (2013–14, 2018–19)
- 2-time Finals MVP (2013–14, 2018–19)
- 2019–20 All-Star Game MVP
- 2-time Defensive Player of the Year (2014–15, 2015–16)
- 6-time All Star

Kawhi Leonard goes for a layup against David Roddy of the Houston Rockets in an April 9, 2025, game.

2015–16 to 2016–17. At the time the only players to have single seasons of at least 23/6/3/1.8 on better than 60 percent True Shooting were Larry Bird, Charles Barkley, Michael Jordan and LeBron James. Leonard finished second in MVP voting in 2015–16, adding another Defensive Player of the Year award, and then finished third in both the MVP and DPOY voting in 2016–17.

But when he couldn't solve the injury to his leg in 2017–18, his relationship with the Spurs fractured and he was traded to the Raptors. It wasn't his choice — his preference was to go back home to Los Angeles — but that didn't affect his performance.

He treaded carefully during the regular season, limiting himself to 60 games to make sure he would be in peak condition — thus introducing the term "load management" into the NBA lexicon. But when the playoffs started, Leonard was at his absolute best. He averaged 30.5 points, 9.1 rebounds and 3.9 assists with a True Shooting percentage of 61.9 — a spectacular level of efficiency against the NBA's best defenses as the Raptors' focal point. He made one of the most iconic shots in league history — forever known in Toronto as "The Shot" — when his buzzer-beating baseline fadeaway took four bounces on the rim before falling in to eliminate the Philadelphia 76ers in a seven-game second-round series. He joined Kareem Abdul-Jabbar and James as the only players to win the Finals MVP for two different teams when he earned the trophy after the Raptors eliminated the Golden State Warriors in six games in the 2019 Finals.

"I told myself I would be back," he said. "I wasn't going to come back until I could be the player I am today ... Just being able to win this championship this year is just something special for me ..."

Leonard signed with the Los Angeles Clippers in free agency in 2019, but the concerns about staying healthy he voiced before joining the Raptors proved prophetic. He managed one fully healthy season with Los Angeles — during the pandemic-interrupted 2019–20 campaign — but the Clippers were eliminated in the second round.

In the years following, Leonard proved both dominant and fragile. Over the first 11 games of the 2020–21 playoffs, he was playing as well as anyone ever has, with averages of 30.4 points, 7.7 rebounds, 4.4 assists and 2.1 steals — postseason numbers only Michael Jordan has ever matched, and never with the level of efficiency indicated by Leonard's 67.9 percent True Shooting mark — before going down with an ACL injury that kept him out for the entire 2021–22 season. He had season-ending knee problems in the 2023 and 2024 playoffs, too.

But at the end of the 2024–25 season, Leonard showed that he still had some high-octane gas in the tank. After missing the first three months of the season making sure his knee was fully recovered, Leonard got up to full speed after the All-Star break, leading the Clippers to a 16-5 record in the games he played, as he averaged 25 points, 7 rebounds, 3.4 assists and 2 steals per game while shooting 52.1 percent from the field and 43.2 percent from three. He was even better in the playoffs as he averaged 25 points, 7.6 rebounds and 4.7 assists on 53.7/40.5 shooting splits as the Clipppers pushed the favored Denver Nuggets to seven games before being eliminated in the first round.

It bodes well for the final stages of what is already a Hall-of-Fame career. With his two championships, two Defensive Player of the Year awards and two Finals MVPs on top of seven All-Defensive teams and six All-NBA teams, his status as one of the greats of his era is assured. But if he can finish his career healthy, he may be able to add a whole new chapter to his legacy. ■

MILWAUKEE BUCKS

POSITION PG // **SHOOTS** RIGHT // **HEIGHT** 6'2" // **WEIGHT** 195 LBS // **DRAFTED** 2012, 6TH OVERALL

Far away, in the Pacific Northwest, a star was born.

It didn't take Damian Lillard long to become one for the Portland Trail Blazers after he was drafted sixth overall in 2012 out of Weber State University, a mid-major school in Utah not known for producing NBA lottery picks.

In the first NBA game Lillard ever played, he scored 23 points and distributed 11 assists, joining Oscar Robertson and Allen Iverson as the only rookies in NBA history to record at least 20 points and 10 assists in their NBA debut. By season's end he became the fourth player in league history to win Rookie of the Year honors by unanimous vote, joining Blake Griffin, David Robinson and Ralph Sampson on the shortlist. The Blazers had won just 28 games before Lillard was drafted and jumped to 33-, 54- and 51-win seasons while he was still on his rookie contract.

Lillard was an All Star in his second and third seasons and made the All-NBA team in his fourth.

And so it became. The 6-foot-2 guard with the buttery change of pace, explosive hops and a seemingly unguardable jump shot became a star in Portland. The Trail Blazers made the playoffs for eight consecutive seasons from 2013–14 through 2020–21, and Lillard finished eighth or better in MVP voting five times.

Only LeBron James, James Harden and Stephen Curry could match Lillard's averages of 25.9 points and 6.7 assists with an effective field goal percentage of 52.5 percent over that eight-year stretch.

Lillard was lightly recruited coming out of the Oakland, California, high school scene and wasn't really on the NBA's radar until a breakout season as a redshirt junior at Weber State. From these humble beginnings, he established himself as NBA royalty, earning a spot on the league's 75th anniversary team in 2021. Lillard also gained a reputation as one of the NBA's coolest customers in the clutch.

"That's just the type of person I am," he said when asked about his calm demeanor under pressure. "There's no reason to be scared out there. It's just a basketball game, so I never get worried or rattled by the situation. If you're going to win, you're going to win. If you're going to lose, you're going to lose. I want to win games, but I'm not affected by any situation. My emotions go up and down like everybody else's, but I don't feel the need to show the world."

The top thing missing from Lillard's glittering résumé is the ultimate prize — an NBA championship, or even the chance to compete

Damian Lillard drives to the basket for an uncontested layup in a December 28, 2024, game against the Chicago Bulls.

for one. Lillard led the Trail Blazers to the Western Conference Finals in 2018–19, but no further. Portland was too good to pick up star-level talent at the top of the draft during Lillard's years there, and attracting free agent help to one of the NBA's smallest and most distant markets was a challenge.

By the 2023–24 offseason, it was clear something had to give. For Lillard, heading into his 12th season, to have a chance to win a championship meant moving on from Portland. For the Trail Blazers to successfully rebuild, they likely needed the type of assets trading a star of Lillard's magnitude could bring.

It all went down in September 2023, when, just before training camp, Lillard woke from a nap to find out he was being traded to the Milwaukee Bucks where he would immediately gain the best teammate he ever had, two-time MVP Giannis Antetokounmpo.

On paper it seemed like the perfect basketball union: one of the most dominant rim-running big men in NBA history working alongside Lillard, one of the craftiest offensive players of his generation.

But it never quite clicked. The Bucks did win 49 games and headed into the playoffs as the East's third seed, and Lillard did average 24.3 points and 7 assists per game and was named an All Star for the eighth time in his career, but his efficiency wasn't up to his usual level. Given the age and stage of their roster, Milwaukee's only acceptable outcome would have been an NBA Finals appearance and a shot at winning the franchise's second championship in four years. But injuries to Antetokounmpo and Lillard come playoff time scuttled those hopes, and the Bucks were eliminated in the first round of the 2023–24 playoffs.

"That whole process was just kind of unsettling," Lillard told ESPN during a midseason interview. "Being away from my kids, being away from my family, there's a lot of things that made it like a more difficult process on the court. That's not the part that people care about, but it's a part of it because it's a part of me.

"Then just getting comfortable having a different role, playing with another star like Giannis, a different style of play, it was a lot of change all at once."

By the time the 2024–25 season rolled around, Lillard, Antetokounmpo and the Bucks were in a much better place. The first indication that things were different came when Milwaukee won the 2024 Emirates NBA Cup.

"I've had a lot of experience individually where I've had accomplishments and stuff," Lillard said after the Bucks defeated the Oklahoma City Thunder in the cup final. "But to have some team success and win something and be the last team standing in this tournament, it feels great."

But misfortune struck Lillard again when, in late March, he was diagnosed with a blood clot in his right calf, which caused him to sit out for the Bucks' remaining 13 games and the first game of Milwaukee's opening-round series against the Indiana Pacers. Lillard was cleared for Game 2, but then he tore his left Achilles tendon early in Game 4. The Bucks lost the series in five games, and with Lillard likely lost for all of the 2025–26 season, Milwaukee took the unusual step of waiving the star guard, making him a free agent. It means that when he recovers from his injury, Lillard will have a chance to choose where to resume his chase for a championship and the crowning achievement of a tremendous career. ■

CAREER HIGHLIGHTS

- 2023–24 All-Star Game MVP
- 2012–13 Rookie of the Year
- 9-time All Star
- 2017–18 All-NBA First Team
- 4-time All-NBA Second Team

CLEVELAND CAVALIERS

45 Donovan

MITCHELL

POSITION SG, PG // **SHOOTS** RIGHT // **HEIGHT** 6'3" // **WEIGHT** 215 LBS // **DRAFTED** 2017, 13TH OVERALL

It takes a special player to change the fortunes of two franchises before even turning 28 years old, but Donovan Mitchell is well on his way to proving himself as one.

He came on the scene as a relatively unheralded No. 13 pick out of Louisville, acquired on draft night by a Utah Jazz team that had won 51 games in 2016–17, had lost in the second round of the playoffs and was reeling from the departure of All-Star forward Gordon Hayward in free agency.

Attracting big-name free agents had never been in the cards for Salt Lake City, a small market offering beautiful mountain views and a quiet lifestyle but little else that might lure stars with eyes for Los Angeles, New York or Miami.

But it didn't take long for Mitchell to make Jazz fans forget Hayward. He went off for 37 points in his NBA Summer League debut, and in his 23rd NBA start he set a franchise record for rookies with a 41-point explosion in a win over the New Orleans Pelicans. In February he won the dunk contest at All-Star weekend, and by season's end he earned All-Rookie First Team honors and finished second in Rookie of the Year voting to Ben Simmons of the Philadelphia 76ers.

He helped the Jazz to the playoffs and back into the second round by scoring 171 points in a six-game series win over the Oklahoma City Thunder — the third-most ever by a rookie in a six-game series, behind only Wilt Chamberlain and Michael Jordan.

It was the start of a spectacular five-year run in Utah, during which he made three All-Star teams and led the Jazz to the playoffs all five years while the team averaged 48-win seasons over that stretch. But Utah couldn't quite get over the top in the postseason, and in the summer of 2022, CEO of basketball operations Danny Ainge signaled it was time to start fresh, trading both Mitchell and Rudy Gobert, Utah's defensive anchor.

After his departure, it was Mitchell, who could deliver 50-point games with both hailstorms of deep threes and thunderous dunks, that the fanbase couldn't help but lament.

"Donovan Mitchell became a star so quickly in Utah that it was literally unbelievable. So many times during his early years on the Jazz, I'd think to myself 'how is this real?' or 'we never get players like this," Taylor Griffin of SLC Dunk, a popular Jazz website, wrote in appreciation after Mitchell

was traded to Cleveland prior to 2022–23. "When Donovan was catching the eyes of guys like LeBron James or Dwyane Wade post-game and they would come up specifically to him, it just felt so surreal. Having a dude that they were actually showing on ESPN highlights was a pretty big deal."

In Cleveland, Mitchell's task was even greater: lift the low-glamor, small-market Cavaliers to heights only LeBron James had ever managed.

Once again, Mitchell proved to be up to the task, using the lessons he'd learned in in his five years with the Jazz to emerge as a leader with the Cavaliers. In his first season with the Cavs, Mitchell reached new heights, averaging a career-best 28.3 points per game to go along with 4.4 assists and 4.3 rebounds while earning All-NBA recognition for the first time.

"I don't know all that he was asked to do when he was in Utah," then-Cavaliers head coach Bernie Bickerstaff said of his new star. "But what I've seen from him is a really complete basketball player. I've seen a guy who's willing to compete on the defensive end at a high level. I've seen a guy who's willing to take challenges on that end of the floor. And I've seen a guy who's been willing over and over again just to make the right pass and make the easy pass, on top of going out and scoring the basketball. I could be wrong. He was in the Western Conference so I didn't see him, but he just seems … he's a better, complete player than I thought, just in the times that I saw him and wasn't able to dissect him. But being around him every day, there's nothing that he's not capable of doing on the basketball court."

But playoff success continued to be elusive. The Mitchell-led Cavaliers were eliminated in the first round in 2022–23 and then the second round in 2023–24 — after another strong regular season — falling in five games to the eventual champion Boston Celtics. It looked like Mitchell and the Cavs were going to have their moment in 2024–25 as Cleveland handily led the Eastern Conference with a 64-18 record and swept aside the over-matched Miami Heat in the first round. But between injuries to three different Cavaliers starters and a superb performance by the Indiana Pacers, Cleveland and Mitchell were bounced in the second round for the third-straight season. Mitchell averaged 34.2 points, 5.8 rebounds, 3.8 assists and 2.2 steals in the series, but for the eighth time in his eight-year career, he saw his playoff run fall short of the conference finals.

Donovan Mitchell shoots over Indiana Pacers guard Andrew Nembhard in Game 5 of the second round of the playoffs on May 13, 2025.

CAREER HIGHLIGHTS

- 6-time All Star
- 2024–25 All-NBA First Team
- 2022–23 All-NBA Second Team
- 2017–18 All-Rookie First Team

"Just couldn't believe it," Mitchell told reporters in Cleveland at the season's end. "Didn't want to believe it, don't want to believe it, still don't want to believe it. It's tough. It's tough to win in this league … So now we gotta use this as motivation. Everybody's gonna write us off, everybody in here. It's not personal, [but] what are we going to do about it next year?"

We'll wait and see. ■

Domantas SABONIS

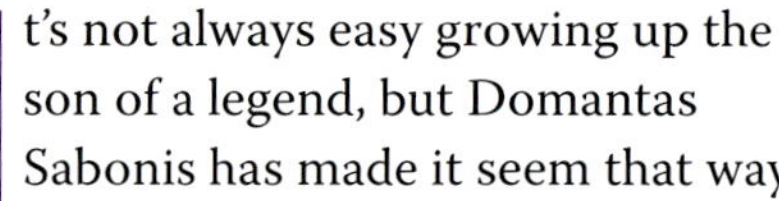

POSITION C, PF // **SHOOTS** LEFT // **HEIGHT** 6'10" // **WEIGHT** 240 LBS // **DRAFTED** 2016, 11TH OVERALL

It's not always easy growing up the son of a legend, but Domantas Sabonis has made it seem that way.

The Sacramento Kings big man has always been known as the son of Arvydas Sabonis, the giant and supremely skilled Lithuanian center who starred in the NBA at the end of his career but whose greatest feats were accomplished as a younger player in Europe before injuries slowed him (and when videos of his exploits were scarce).

But year by year his youngest son, Domantas, has carved out a career and reputation that can stand alone.

The Sacramento Kings star has amassed his own list of unique accomplishments.

There was his "perfect game" on November 6, 2024, when, against the Toronto Raptors, Sabonis became the first player in NBA history to have a triple double (17-13-11) without missing either a field goal attempt or a free throw and without making a turnover.

There were his NBA-record 77 double-doubles he tallied during the 2023–24 season. He also set an NBA record for consecutive double-doubles that season, as he finished with 65 straight, something he accomplished while appearing in all 82 games for Sacramento and finishing second in the NBA in minutes played.

"It's crazy, man, just the consistency," said then-Kings teammate De'Aaron Fox. "He goes out there every night, he plays hard, he does what he needs to do, what we need him to do, he's willing to do anything to win a basketball game."

He has two rebounding titles and is one of five players to have at least 25 triple-doubles in a season, joining a list that includes Oscar Robertson, Wilt Chamberlain, Nikola Jokic and Russell Westbrook.

Since being drafted 11th overall out of Gonzaga University and playing for the Oklahoma City Thunder and the Indiana Pacers before landing in Sacramento during the 2021–22 season, Sabonis has racked up three All-Star appearances and two All-NBA nominations.

For Sabonis, it's all quite literally a dream come true.

When his father was playing in Portland from 1995 through 2003, young Sabonis would have the run of the Trail Blazers' locker room and practice facility, enjoying the perks of life in the NBA.

"I remember we would go into the practice facility and, like, try every single Gatorade, and the players would get mad, like 'who's out here taking sips out of every single color of Gatorade?' and it's just three little blond kids running around," Sabonis said on an appearance on the *Rich Eisen Show*.

Sometimes it's difficult to live up to a family legacy, but Sabonis always wanted to follow in his father's footsteps.

"Always, since I was a kid, I wanted to play basketball, that's all I cared about," he said in the same interview. "It was the only sport I grew up playing ... it's amazing, having my dad to go back and forth with, he's been through it all, so I can ask him questions, so it helps a lot."

The younger Sabonis seems to have plenty of answers, honestly.

He's emerged as one of the most skilled big men in league history, a status that would likely be better known if he didn't happen to play in the shadow of Nikola Jokic, the Denver Nuggets star who also puts up triple-doubles on a near-nightly basis and has expanded the definition of the role a center can play.

But Sabonis can more than hold his own. Since his first All-Star season in 2019–20, he's the only player in the NBA to average at least 19 points, 12 rebounds and 6 assists. Only nine players in that period averaged at least 19 points and 6 assists, and of them only Jokic shot more efficiently than Sabonis, who had an effective field goal mark of 59.8 percent.

Not surprisingly, Sabonis' level of play translated to team success, in particular leading Sacramento to the playoffs in 2022–23, breaking the Kings' 16-year playoff drought, which was the longest in NBA history. Sabonis went on to have two more superb individual seasons. In 2023–24 he averaged 19.4 points, a league-leading 13.7 rebounds and a career-best 8.2 assists, as he made the All-NBA team for the second time. The Kings won a respectable 46 games but lost in the play-in tournament. In 2024–25 Sabonis became the first player in league history to average at least 19 points, 13 rebounds, 6 assists and shoot 40 percent from three — his 41.7 percent mark a career-high — but in the highly competitive Western Conference, the Kings slipped to 40 wins and lost the play-in for a second year.

Domantas Sabonis rises past the Oklahoma City Thunder's Kenrich Williams in a game on February 1, 2025, in Oklahoma City.

CAREER HIGHLIGHTS

- 3-time All Star
- 2-time All-NBA Third Team
- 3-time Rebounding Champion (2022–23, 2023–24, 2024–25)

Sabonis has continued to build on his varied strengths throughout his career. In the paint and at the rim, he's proven to be one of the strongest players in the league, able to fight for position and work tenaciously to get to his preferred left hand, regardless of what the defense is doing. He's a superb ball handler and agile, so he is perfectly comfortable pulling down defensive rebounds and leading the fast break himself. In the half court he's an expert screener and a threat to either keep the ball and score or create space for his teammates to use to their advantage.

It's no surprise that when DeMar DeRozan, a six-time All Star with a career 21-point scoring average, joined the Kings for the 2024–25 season, he instantly formed a chemistry with Sabonis.

"Having a high-IQ big like that setting screens, passing the ball, making quick decisions, you can't guard it," said DeRozan of the two-man game between him and his new teammate. "The defense has to make a decision, and there's just so many options you play out of it, it makes it tough on the defense."

There are few players in the NBA today who make life tougher on opposing defenses than Sabonis.

As great as his father was internationally and in the NBA, the son has built his own legacy based on consistency and excellence that stands on its own. ■

NEW YORK KNICKS

Karl-Anthony TOWNS

POSITION C, PF // **SHOOTS** RIGHT // **HEIGHT** 7'0" // **WEIGHT** 248 LBS // **DRAFTED** 2015, 1ST OVERALL

Karl-Anthony Towns powers to the rim in a March 7, 2025, game against the Los Angeles Clippers.

Partway through the 2021–22 NBA season, Karl-Anthony Towns made one of those statements you can't walk back, that leaves little room for interpretation and that follows you, for good or bad.

The then-Minnesota Timberwolves star gave himself a title, as clearly as if he were strapping on an oversized gold belt, like a boastful championship wrestler.

"I'm the greatest big man shooter of all time. That's a fact," Towns said in an interview with Jon Krawczynski of *The Athletic* that quickly went viral. "You can see the stats. I ain't got to play like no one else. Everyone trying to find themselves to be the second version of me when I'm the first version. I don't got to be the second version of someone else. I'm already an original. I don't have to be a duplicate of someone else."

Towns had a case, even then. Through his first five NBA seasons, the No. 1–overall pick out of the University of Kentucky already had one hand on the belt. Already a two-time All Star and the 2015–16 Rookie of the Year, Towns' career three-point shooting mark was 39.6 percent, just a hair below the 40-percent mark that designates elite shooters. Among 7-footers, only Dallas Mavericks legend and Hall of Famer Dirk Nowitzki could compare. Nowitzki retired after 21 seasons as one of six players to have scored 30,000 points in his career, and as the career leader for 7-footers in three-point attempts and three-point makes. He was joined only by Channing Frye for having shot at least 38 percent from deep on a minimum of 1,000 career attempts.

When Towns made his comment, he was coming off three-straight years of cracking the 40 percent threshold. During the 2019–20 season Towns was in the midst of one of the best shooting seasons anyone had ever had to that point — 41.2 percent on nearly 8 attempts per game — before injuries limited his season to 35 starts. For context,

CAREER HIGHLIGHTS

- > 2015–16 Rookie of the Year
- > 5-time All Star
- > 3-time All-NBA Third Team
- > 2015–16 All-Rookie First Team

when Stephen Curry was an All Star for the first time in 2013–14 he shot 42.4 percent on his 7.9 attempts per game, which at the time was the second-most prolific season for made-threes in league history.

To his credit, once Towns put the words out there, he didn't shy away from backing them up.

After years of "begging" the NBA to accept him into the three-point contest on All-Star weekend, he got his chance in 2022 and won it, prompting him to post on X, "I told ya," and later telling reporters, "[I'm] just tremendously confident in my shooting ability ... I wanted to keep pressure on everybody, get a high number [of makes] that makes it feel almost unattainable." His 29-point final-round score set a new record.

Towns' shooting range, and his ability to make threes from all areas of the floor and on the move, is perhaps his standout offensive skill, but it's far from his only one. Towns combines his ability to stretch the defense with his post-up skills and knack for long-legged physical drives that send bodies flying and rack up fouls, making him one of the most difficult matchups in the NBA.

The pairing of size, scoring instincts and skill made Towns the Rookie of the Year, after which NBA general managers named Towns the young player they would pick to build a franchise around. For an encore Towns put up 25.1 points, 12.3 rebounds and blocked 1.3 shots with a True Shooting percentage of 61.8, making him one of just five players to hit all those marks in one year and the only one to do it at age 23 or younger — Towns being just 21 at the time. Later in his career Towns also went on to be one of just nine NBA players to twice score at least 60 points in a game.

His production in Minnesota never wavered and four All-Star nods followed, along with earning All-NBA recognition on two occasions. But team success was harder to realize, with Towns' defensive shortcomings often tabbed as a contributing factor. Still, the Timberwolves made the playoffs three times in Towns' first eight seasons, losing in the first round each time. However, when they finally punched through and advanced to the Western Conference Finals in 2023–24, the Timberwolves found themselves in a tight spot financially with three players — Towns, Anthony Edwards and Rudy Gobert — on max contracts. In the end it was Towns who was the odd man out as he was traded to the New York Knicks on the eve of the 2024–25 season, reuniting him with his old head coach from Minnesota, Tom Thibodeau.

"These guys have something special here," Towns said upon joining the Knicks. "... I'm here to help and be the best teammate that I can be."

If there was any concern the bright lights of Manhattan would be too much for the New Jersey native, Towns put those aside quickly as he averaged 24.4 points, 12.8 rebounds and 3 assists for the Knicks. Towns earned All-NBA Third Team honors and the Knicks won 51 games and finished third in the Eastern Conference before losing out to the Indiana Pacers in six games in the conference finals — the Knicks' deepest postseason run in 25 years.

Oh, and Towns shot 42 percent from the three-point line, the best by any center in the league with at least 250 attempts from deep. ■

NEW ORLEANS PELICANS

1 Zion WILLIAMSON

POSITION PF // **SHOOTS** LEFT // **HEIGHT** 6'6" // **WEIGHT** 284 LBS // **DRAFTED** 2019, 1ST OVERALL

The entire Zion Williamson NBA experience can be encapsulated in a single game in April 2024.

The New Orleans Pelicans were trailing the Los Angeles Lakers by 11 points with 7:38 to play in the fourth quarter of the first game of the play-in tournament, the last-chance route for teams trying to qualify for the NBA playoffs.

The Pelicans were having a hard time scoring. Their four starters not named Williamson ended up shooting just 13-of-43 from the field, or a fraction over 30.2 percent.

And then Williamson checked back in the game.

By that point in his career, the perception of Williamson, who was drafted first overall in 2019, had already shifted from a player who might end up as the NBA's next generational superstar to something of an enigma. No one has ever doubted his talent, but counting on him was a fool's errand. Even by the end of the 2023–24 season, in which he played a career-high 70 games, he had still missed more games (216) than he had played (184) in his then-five-year career.

When he played he was incredible, combining a level of quickness, elusiveness, explosiveness and skill never before seen in a 6-foot-6, 284-pound package.

From the moment Williamson came into the NBA as the most-hyped prospect since LeBron James, he had shown his ability to dominate games at the highest levels of competition — if his precarious health allowed.

In his first 100 NBA games Williamson averaged 26.2 points a game on 60 percent shooting, a level of productivity and efficiency unmatched by any other player in league history through their first 100 games. The catch? Williamson didn't play his 100th game until his fourth season.

But in his fifth season it looked like things might finally be coming together for Williamson and the Pelicans. He set a career-high in games played (70) and averaged 22.9 points, 5.8 rebounds and 5 assists on 57 percent shooting — only three-time MVP Nikola Jokic and two-time MVP Giannis Antetokounmpo averaged those thresholds or better in 2023–24. Not coincidentally, the Pelicans won 49 games, tied for second-best in franchise history and the most in 15 years.

But there they were in the first round of the play-in tournament, and down by double figures on their homecourt with time slipping away.

As soon as Williamson checked in, he instantly grabbed a defensive rebound, dribbled the length of the floor and slithered his massive frame to the rim for a layup. Then he contested LeBron James at the rim, ran the floor and set up his teammate Jose Alvarado for a triple. The crowd in New Orleans was hyped. They were even more so when Williamson cut the baseline and elevated his giant frame for an alley-oop dunk. The Lakers' lead was two. A moment later Williamson snuck out on the fast break and buried another alley-oop to tie the game. The Lakers took the lead again, but Williamson had the ball and was dribbling in isolation against Anthony Davis, one of the best defenders in the sport. The Pelicans star seemed unbothered as he dribbled hard right before pulling up for a floater, which he made.

The game was tied again with 3:19 to play, but after hitting that floater, Williamson started moving awkwardly. He was in pain. He got subbed out on the next play and pulled a towel over his head and walked back to the Pelicans' locker room, the picture of dejection.

He had good reason to be upset. Williamson finished with 40 points, 11 rebounds, 5 assists, a block and a steal on 17-of-27 shooting in a crucial game, but he got hurt and the Pelicans lost by four.

"[He was] fantastic," Pelicans head coach Willie Green said of his star-crossed star. "He settled into the game. He just continued to attack. He found seams. He rebounded the ball. He played fast … [If] we have him for a few more minutes, maybe we have a chance to pull this thing out."

The Pelicans did make the playoffs, but Williamson didn't, his season ended by a hamstring injury. New Orleans lost in four games to the Oklahoma City Thunder, closing the book on another disappointing season, spoiled in part by their star's injury problems.

The following year brought more frustration as another hamstring strain saw Williamson shut down after playing just six games to start the 2024–25 season. He eventually played just 30 games for the year, bringing his career total to just 214 of a possible 472 games, or 45.3 percent over his first six seasons. As always when he was on the floor, there were flashes of brilliance: 31 points and 3 blocks on 13-of-18 shooting in 31 minutes against the Toronto Raptors one night, 40 points on 16-of-21 shooting in 27 minutes against Sacramento on another — but the Pelicans, their season decimated by injuries to Williamson and others, finished with a 21-61 record and were back in the lottery again.

And the question around Williamson remained the same as ever: would he ever stay healthy enough to take his place among the game's greats? ■

Zion Williamson dunks in a game against the Minnesota Timberwolves on March 19, 2025.

CAREER HIGHLIGHTS

- 2-time All Star
- 2019–20 All-Rookie First Team

THE GOLDEN AGE OF PARITY

Let's hear it for the losers. The close-but-no-cigar crowd and the woulda, coulda, shouldas.

Let's pour one out for the 2023–24 Dallas Mavericks, the 2022–23 Miami Heat and the 2020–21 Phoenix Suns — teams that made it to the NBA Finals when no one was necessarily expecting it and disappeared from championship contention almost as quickly as they got there.

Let's acknowledge that in a 30-team NBA with talent spread liberally across the league, winning an NBA championship is harder than it's ever been and that just being in the hunt is a feat worth celebrating.

After decades of a superstar's worthiness being judged by whether they had a championship to their name or not, or of a team only being fully appreciated if they won it all, let's come to an understanding that, sure, standing at center court with confetti raining down is a wonderful, beautiful thing that should be celebrated. But using that as the only measure of greatness is a hollow, frustrating way to appreciate the best basketball has to offer.

The NBA seems to agree.

Welcome, friends, to the golden age of parity.

There was a time when the Russells, Kareems, Birds, Magics and Jordans ruled the league, eventually passing their crowns off to the Duncans, Shaqs, Kobes, LeBrons and Currys.

Together those 10 one-namers played on teams that won 42 of the NBA's last 69 titles.

Of the thousands of NBA players over decades of competition, teams

LeBron James receives the Bill Russell NBA Finals Most Valuable Player trophy from legend Bill Russell following the Heat's victory against the San Antonio Spurs in the 2013 NBA Finals. Between James and Russell, they have 15 championships.

The Toronto Raptors celebrate after they defeated the Golden State Warriors in Game 6 of the 2019 NBA Finals. Their victory kicked off a seven-year run during which no NBA champions were repeat winners.

with those 10 walked away with the trophy more than 60 percent of the time.

The concentration of championships is even more pronounced when calculated by franchise. Five teams — the Lakers, Celtics, Warriors, Bulls and Spurs — have won 53 championships, with the rest of the NBA combining for 26 through the league's first 79 seasons. If we expand the list to include organizations with three titles — the Heat, Pistons and 76ers — it's 62 of 79.

But that level of dominance seems like it could be a thing of the past. When the Toronto Raptors won the NBA championship in 2018–19, becoming one of just eight teams in league history to win a single NBA title, it began a seven-year run during which the NBA didn't have a repeat champion — the longest stretch in league history.

And while there was some familiarity among the winners during that stretch — Steph Curry and the Golden State Warriors won the fourth title of Curry's career in 2021–22, and the Boston Celtics won their NBA-record 18th championship in 2023–24 — there were some new faces, too: the Raptors, of course, but also the 2020–21 Milwaukee Bucks, which won their first title in 50 years, and the 2022–23 Denver Nuggets, which won for the first time in what, at the time, was their 46-year history. In 2024–25 the Oklahoma City Thunder iteration of the franchise joined the ranks of the first-time champions with their Finals win over the Indiana Pacers, who were also looking for their first NBA title. In the Western Conference Finals, the Thunder defeated the Minnesota Timberwolves as they sought the first championship in their 36-year history, and in the east the Pacers upset the Knicks, who were looking for their first championship since 1973.

Is it a blip, a pause in time before the next dynasty comes roaring back? Or has something fundamentally shifted with how the NBA operates and teams are built? There are exceptions to every rule, and exceptions to

Draymond Green and LeBron James have words during Game 4 of the 2016 NBA Finals. This moment could be seen as a turning point that precipitated the arrival of Kevin Durant to the Bay Area.

exceptions, but there is at least some sense that things have changed.

"I think the one thing the NBA has done a good job of is creating parity in the league," former Toronto Raptors president Masai Ujiri, the architect of the 2019 NBA champion Raptors and two-time NBA executive of the year, remarked on the eve of the 2024–25 playoffs. "I remember in the league a few years ago you could win 50 games, 51 games, 55 games, it didn't matter what you were doing, [Los Angeles Lakers star] Kobe Bryant was coming to kick your ass. Or the Spurs were coming to kick your ass. Or LeBron James in Miami and Dwyane Wade and those guys, they were coming to kick your ass. Or Kevin Garnett and those guys [with the Celtics], they were coming to kick your butt. But now, I don't know, do we know who is going to win the NBA this season? I don't think we do. Celtics [which ended up being upset in the second round by the Knicks] are one of the best teams, they're the defending champions, we give them their respect, but there's been six different winners or so since we won it and I think the system that's created that in the NBA."

NBA history is replete with turning points and moments that helped shape the trajectory of the league and the sport. The introduction of the 24-second clock in 1954–55, the three-point line in 1979–80, and the ascendance of Michael Jordan coinciding with the globalization of the sport in the late 1980s and 1990s all come to mind. But the sequence of events that flowed from Draymond Green hitting LeBron James in the nether regions in Game 4 of the 2016 NBA Finals may be as far reaching and instant as any of them.

Not following? Let me try and explain. The Warriors were leading James and the Cavaliers by 10 points with 2:42 to play and were about to go ahead 3-1 in the best-of-seven Finals. James and Green got tangled up briefly, with Green falling to the floor at James' feet at the three-point line. In an attempt to get back into the play, James steps over Green and the Warriors forward takes offense, getting up and making a flick with his right hand at James' groin area, and the pair get tangled up again, exchanging words. The two are separated, assessed a personal foul and the game goes on. The Warriors win and find themselves on the brink of perhaps the greatest season in NBA history, as they are one win away from capping off their record-setting 73-9 regular season with a championship, which would have been their second straight at that stage.

The only problem was that when the NBA reviewed the play after the game it was determined that Green's flick at James' groin was worthy of a flagrant 1 foul, assessed after the fact. Since it was Green's fourth flagrant foul of the Warriors' postseason run, he was automatically suspended for Game 5. Instead of the Warriors closing out their miracle season with their second-straight title, the Cavaliers won Game 5 with Green out, won Game 6 at home in Cleveland to tie the series and stole Game 7 at Oracle Arena — the win hinging on James' iconic chase-down block on Andre Iguodala and Kyrie Irving's game-winning jumper, with James completing his hero's journey and delivering a championship to Cleveland.

What happened next?

Green reaches out to Kevin Durant of the Oklahoma City Thunder and recruits him to join the Warriors. Would Durant have come to Golden State if they were twice-defending champs? Would the Warriors have felt the need to make such a momentous change? That's unknown, but Durant allowed the possibility when asked about it shortly after signing with the Warriors that summer.

"We don't have to talk about it because they didn't get the job done and they came after me," Durant said. "Who knows what would have happened. But I guess you could say I'm glad they lost."

What happened next requires no speculation. The Warriors, featuring a lineup of Curry, Klay Thompson, Green and Durant proved almost unbeatable, racing to the next two NBA titles, accumulating a 32-5 postseason record. They went 8-1 in back-to-back Finals against James and the Cavaliers, before the Durant-era Warriors were brought down by devastating injuries to Durant and Thompson during the 2019 Finals against the Raptors.

What made the Warriors' run of dominance possible, however, also happened off the floor. As the NBA continued to grow in popularity, it became an increasingly valuable product for broadcasters and media companies trying to reach the NBA audience. So much so that beginning in the 2016–17 season, the league's media rights deal jumped from about $1.06 billion per year to $2.67 billion. Since the league shares roughly half of its basketball related income with the players, the effect on salaries was immediate, with the salary cap — the amount teams are allowed to spend on their rosters — jumping from $70 million to $94 million, the largest year-over-year increase in league history (the increase the year before had been less than $7 million).

It's an oversimplification to say that what became known as the "cap spike" was the only reason the Warriors were able to add Durant and his $27 million salary as a free agent without having to give up any of their star-laden core — the Warriors had been planning for several years to have cap space available in the summer of 2016 and

Kevin Durant holds the Finals MVP award after the Golden State Warriors defeated the Cleveland Cavaliers in the 2017 NBA Finals.

benefitted from having two-time defending MVP Steph Curry on the below-market contract he signed when he was coming off ankle surgery. But the reality remains: a 73-win team was able to add an all-time great in free agency because of a one-time financial event.

Even more troubling for some corners of the NBA, the Warriors were able to keep that team together. All it cost was money. Because the NBA's collective bargaining agreement (CBA) allows teams to exceed the cap to re-sign their own players, the Warriors were able to keep rolling even as the players' individual salaries continued to climb. At the end of the 2016–17 season Curry signed a five-year deal for $201 million. By the end of the 2018–19 season the Warriors' overall payroll — including a $51.5 million tax bill — was $197 million. The NBA has always had mechanisms designed to reign in profligate spenders. Teams that cross certain salary thresholds are hit with increasingly punitive "luxury tax"' payments, but the cost of winning doesn't seem to deter a certain class of owners. When the Warriors won their fourth championship of the Curry era in 2021–22, their payroll, including luxury tax payments, was $346.2 million. In contrast, when Shaquille O'Neal and Kobe Bryant led the Los Angeles Lakers to the last of the three titles they won together 20 years earlier, the Lakers' total payroll was $54.3 million.

And league-wide a pattern was emerging in which a handful of owners were stacking salaries in order to stack teams good enough to compete with the standard the Warriors had set. The Los Angeles Clippers, under the ownership of multibillionaire Steve Ballmer, the league's wealthiest owner, spent $923.3 million in salaries and luxury tax payments between 2021–22 and 2023–24 to build and keep together a team that could win a championship. The Milwaukee Bucks spent $711 million over the same three-year period trying to maintain a championship-level team following their title win in 2021. The Warriors kept the taps open, spending $1.08 billion combined in 2021–22, 2022–23 and 2023–24.

It was an unsustainable model, both for the teams unwilling or unable to spend hundreds of millions of dollars in payroll penalties to compete and for some of the teams writing the cheques.

"As an owner of a franchise, you're always trying to win. But there's a cost to it," former Milwaukee Bucks owner Marc Lasry said to *GQ Sports* shortly after selling his 25 percent share of the team for an estimated $800 million in 2023. "And the question is, what are you willing to spend? And I think that's different for every owner ... If you can constantly find people who are willing to [spend] that's great. But it's hard for people to fund losses. It just is. Most people act in their economic interests. So I think for [the Bucks owners], we ended up losing money, because we were in the luxury tax. But at the same time, we wanted to win. So we tried to do everything possible to win."

The NBA listened, it seemed. The league introduced several changes to the collective bargaining agreement with the players' association that took effect for the 2023–24 season. Among the most significant were far-reaching penalties for teams that spent above and beyond the luxury tax threshold. Whereas before the consequences were mainly financial, going forward teams that consistently overspend risk being unable to use future draft picks in trades or having a pick moved to the bottom of the first round. As well teams that are above the "second apron" have more restrictions placed on them when it comes to making trades. It forces teams to make difficult decisions: In the summer of 2024, the Denver Nuggets didn't re-sign veteran wing Kentavious Caldwell-Pope — a crucial starter on their 2022–23 championship team — because they didn't want to face the tax penalties and roster-building restrictions that would have followed. The Los Angeles Clippers chose not to re-sign Paul George. The Minnesota Timberwolves celebrated their run to the 2024 Western Conference Finals — their most successful season in 20 years — by trading franchise cornerstone Karl-Anthony Towns a few months later to gain future financial flexibility as they try to build a championship-contending team around Anthony Edwards. Meanwhile quality veteran players on big contracts have proven to be increasingly difficult to trade as fewer teams are in position to acquire them because of second-apron restrictions.

It was all part of a plan, according to NBA commissioner Adam Silver.

"In this league, superstar players are still going to win a disproportionate number of championships, and well-managed franchises are still going to win a disproportionate number of championships," Silver said. "Where I thought it wasn't good for the game and it wasn't good for the league, that there was no question that there's a correlation between spending and the quality of the team, and that while I understand that dynasties are something that fans will get behind, at the same time what you hear from fans is they want those teams to be created the right way. So people aren't that interested in seeing teams buy championships, so to speak."

As well, the money offers no guarantee of success. None of the league's biggest spenders — the Warriors, Clippers or Bucks — made it to an NBA Finals in the three seasons after Golden State's title in 2022. And the

Oklahoma City Thunder players hold up the Larry O'Brien Championship Trophy after their Game 7 victory against the Indiana Pacers on June 22, 2025.

three franchises won just two playoff series among them.

Have the changes designed to curb spending worked?

It might be too early to judge. In the NBA trends tend to play out over years, if not decades, but there is some evidence that the competitive landscape in the NBA is more wide-open than ever.

"I don't want to say nothing is lost, but to me, I don't think our system, by definition, will prevent repeat championships," Silver said prior to the 2024–25 season. "I think that, yes, it makes it less likely, but we didn't set out to say, 'Let's make sure there's a different champion every year.' I think, again, it goes more to equality of opportunity."

After generations of the roll call of NBA champions being dominated by a small handful of franchises, typically in the league's largest or most desirable markets, the two best regular-season teams in the NBA in 2024–25 were the Cleveland Cavaliers and the Oklahoma City Thunder. Their excellence — the Cavaliers went 64-18 in the regular season and the Thunder 68-14 — was built not by signing high-profile free agents or spending lavish amounts of luxury tax dollars, but by executing well in the draft and finding key players in unexpected places. Evan Mobley was the No. 3–overall pick in the 2021 draft and helped elevate the Cavaliers from a good playoff team to a championship contender when he blossomed into an All Star and NBA Defensive Player of the Year in 2024–25. The Cavs swung big on a trade for six-time All Star Donovan Mitchell, but they were lifted over the top by the likes of Ty Jerome, a journeyman guard they signed for $4.6 million over two years who averaged 12.5 points, 3.4 assists and 1.1 steals while shooting 51 percent from the floor and 43.9 percent from three while finishing third in the voting for Sixth Man of the Year. And for all of that, the league's penchant for parity struck in the second round as Cleveland was upset by another small-market team built patiently through the draft and wise trades, the Indiana Pacers.

Meanwhile the Thunder have assembled what could be the NBA's next dynasty not only with astute trades (like acquiring 2025 NBA MVP Shai Gilgeous-Alexander in a deal with the Clippers in the summer of 2019) but also with smart drafting (they were able to get 2025 All-Star Jalen Williams with the 12th pick in the 2022 draft) and patient player development (they signed All-Defensive forward Lu Dort as an undrafted free agent). It was only after earning the first seed in the Western Conference in 2023–24 with a 57-win season — losing to eventual NBA finalists Dallas in the second round — that the Thunder dipped into the free-agent market, signing veteran big man Isaiah Hartenstein to beef up their front court.

But heading into the 2024–25 season, while Cleveland and OKC were among the leading considered contenders, they had plenty of company. According to preseason projections 11 teams were judged to have a 30-1 chance or better at an NBA title; the season before, in 2023–24, there were 12 teams with a 25-1 or better chance. In comparison, the season before Durant's first year with the Warriors in 2016–17, Golden State was a better-than-even favorite to win the title, the Cavaliers were slightly better than 4-1, while the San Antonio Spurs were next best at 9.25-1. The Boston Celtics — 29-1 — were the only other team better than 30-1.

Having more than a third of the franchises start a season with realistic hopes to compete for the top prize is a departure for a league that has forged so much of its identity and myth around legendary teams and players that fought for championships and carved out their place in league history with titles — leaving little room for anyone else.

But it also holds the promise of more great basketball, not less. And with the way the league has set things up, it also means that greatness will likely be more temporary and spread among more teams for shorter windows of time.

"This game should be celebrated," Los Angeles Lakers head coach JJ Redick said early during the 2024–25 season. "The league is more talented and skilled than it was 18 years ago when I was drafted. That's a fact. There are more players that are excellent. There are more teams that are excellent.

"I heard when I played for, I don't know four or five years, 'Well, why do we even play the regular season? We know who's going to be in the Finals.' Well, guess what? We have parity now ..."

Durant, the 15-time All Star and two-time Finals MVP, whose signing with the Warriors in 2016 may have inadvertently kicked the parity push into gear, knows it firsthand. His 2024–25 Phoenix Suns missed the playoffs despite a star-driven lineup and a league-high $366.6 million payroll. Still, when he stepped back, he saw good things, telling *The Athletic* this:

"I think we're at the peak of basketball, in my opinion ... Obviously, nothing's perfect, and there's going to be complaints from different sides, with people wanting to see it in different ways. But for the most part, you're seeing the growth. You're seeing the players get better. You see it through, what, the last six champions have been different ... I think the game's in a good place." ■

DEFENDERS

Rudy Gobert
GOLDEN STATE WARRIORS
23
Rakuten
Draymond Green

MIAMI HEAT

13

Bam ADEBAYO

POSITION C, PF // **SHOOTS** RIGHT // **HEIGHT** 6'9" // **WEIGHT** 255 LBS // **DRAFTED** 2017, 14TH OVERALL

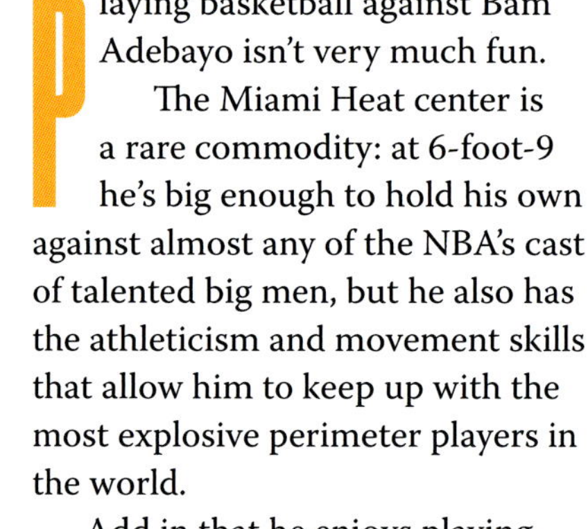

Playing basketball against Bam Adebayo isn't very much fun.

The Miami Heat center is a rare commodity: at 6-foot-9 he's big enough to hold his own against almost any of the NBA's cast of talented big men, but he also has the athleticism and movement skills that allow him to keep up with the most explosive perimeter players in the world.

Add in that he enjoys playing defense and takes satisfaction in making life difficult for the most offensively gifted players in the NBA, and you have a walking, talking misery machine — a basketball joy stealer.

"Every time Bam switched out on us it wasn't going to be easy, you got to move the ball," said Terry Rozier, who played against Adebayo for years before joining him as a teammate in 2023–24. "You probably could run it out, get the switch and then swing it around and try to get the mismatch with the big and the guard ... but I know one thing, it ain't easy for no guard in this league to attack Bam."

The only thing missing from his career to date has been the ultimate recognition as the game's best defender.

"That's one thing that irks me, it's not my fault I'm versatile," Adebayo said while playing for Team USA at the Paris Olympics. "I've been top five in [Defensive Player of the Year] voting the last five years, [but] there's been guys [that voters] have been giving it to over me."

He's correct in that. Adebayo has been a fixture on the NBA's All-Defensive teams since his third season with Miami but has only been on the First Team once, when he finished a career-best third in DPOY voting for the 2023–24 season.

The Miami Heat center has a strong argument that for all the recognition he has earned to this point in his career, he's still underrated.

Former Heat teammate Udonis Haslem — no slouch as a defender himself at his prime — makes the point in plain terms.

"Defensively, who do you know that plays [center] that you can start off on [Boston Celtics star wings] Jaylen Brown or Jayson Tatum in a game?" Haslem said on a podcast during the 2023–24 playoffs. "We started Bam on Jaylen Brown one game and Jayson Tatum in another game in the playoffs"

That versatility and effectiveness is crucial in the modern NBA, where the best way to thwart pick-and-roll actions — the most common offensive

Bam Adebayo defends against Charles Bassey of the San Antonio Spurs in a February 1, 2025, game.

approach in the league, designed to create matchup advantages either in the paint or on the perimeter and generate open threes when a second defender has to help — is by switching. If the player guarding the person setting the screen can simply slide over and guard the ball handler, it takes away one of the primary options for the offense. But few NBA big men are comfortable guarding elite ball handlers outside the paint.

Adebayo is the exception, and the Heat take advantage of that with a switch-heavy defensive scheme that sees the former University of Kentucky star defend opponents other than centers on nearly half of the Heat's defensive possessions, according to BBall Index. He ranks at the very top of the statistical site's measures in categories like perimeter isolation defense, ball-screen navigation and off-ball chaser defense, highlighting his rare ability as a center to guard smaller players away from the basket without help from his teammates.

The eye test is even more convincing. A search of Adebayo's defensive highlights brings moment after moment of the Heat star simply ruining attempts by the best players in the game to make even the most rudimentary plays.

Whether it's sliding down the lane while guarding nine-time All-Star point guard Damian Lillard before finally blocking him at the rim, forcing Luka Doncic into an awkward miss or snatching the ball from emerging star Victor Wembanyama, there are seemingly no plays Adebayo can't make.

Accordingly, the Heat have been ranked in the top 10 defensively from 2020–21 onward.

And he rises to the occasion, too. In 2023–24 as Nikola Jokic was cruising to his third NBA MVP award, one of the few teams he'd stumble against was the Heat, as Adebayo helped hold the Nuggets star to 15 points a game on 47.8 percent shooting, compared to his season averages of 26.4 points a game on 58.3 percent shooting.

CAREER HIGHLIGHTS

- 3-time All Star
- 2023–24 All-Defensive First Team
- 4-time All-Defensive Second Team

"When you talk about versatility, when you talk about a two-way defender," said 14-year NBA veteran and longtime Miami Heat assistant coach Caron Butler, "I mean it's a crime that he hasn't won Defensive Player of the Year."

Bam would agree.

Adebayo narrowly missed being named to the All-Defensive team for the sixth-straight year in 2024–25 as the Heat struggled for most of the season before being eliminated in the first round of the playoffs. However, given he only just turned 28 ahead of his eighth NBA season in 2025–26, there is still plenty of time for him to earn the recognition he believes he deserves. ■

NEW YORK KNICKS

8 OG

ANUNOBY

POSITION SF, PF // **SHOOTS** RIGHT // **HEIGHT** 6'7" // **WEIGHT** 232 LBS // **DRAFTED** 2017, 23RD OVERALL

The NBA is a league that has always prioritized offense. That's what sells tickets, draws in TV viewers and, frankly, is easier to talk about for the chattering classes that cover the league.

But it's difficult to win without elite defense. No one is going to individually stop the best basketball players in the world from scoring, but there are a handful of examples when a single defender can make the best players' lives very, very difficult.

Which brings us to OG Anunoby, one of the few players in the NBA who can credibly match up with everyone from the league's best centers to its craftiest point guards.

Standing at 6-foot-7 with a wingspan that stretches well over 7 feet, weighing in at a rock-solid 232 pounds and yet possessing remarkable quickness, Anunoby can physically stand in against the likes of Nikola Jokic or Joel Embiid in the NBA's heavyweight division, while still chasing around guards and wings.

"Have you seen his legs? You mention his size. But that guy is strong," Denver Nuggets then-head coach Mike Malone said before his team was getting ready to match up against Anunoby late in the 2022–23 season. "When you look at OG guard, whether it is Nikola [Jokic] or anything else, the strength, the athleticism, the IQ, the anticipation, and all great defenders have a common characteristic no matter how they're built — mindset. He has a mindset to go out there and shut down whoever he's guarding."

Anunoby approaches his craft with a meticulous eye for detail, studying his opponents' tendencies and understanding his own team's game plan. But then he reacts and lets his abilities take over.

"If you think too much, you lose your instincts, and if you're all instincts you get erratic," Anunoby told the *Toronto Star* during 2022–23, when he led the NBA in steals. "It's kind of knowing when to gamble and when not to gamble. Sometimes I gamble at the wrong time, or I don't gamble at the time I could have gambled.

"You have to live with it, but it's also just knowing when I can live with it, knowing time and place."

The defensive playmaking is a bonus, but Anunoby's man-to-man defense is where he does his best work. His list of victims is long and illustrious. There was a remarkable stretch late in the 2023–24 season with the Toronto Raptors when Anunoby ruined games for some of the best scorers in the sport. According to NBA tracking data,

All Stars DeMar DeRozan (3 points), Bradley Beal (6 points combined over two games), Jokic (2 points), Kawhi Leonard (9 points) and Anthony Davis (4 points) scored just 24 total points over six games with Anunoby as the primary defender.

Being able to disrupt the NBA's best players is a difference-making attribute, and for most of his career since being drafted 23rd overall out of Indiana University — lower than he otherwise might have been had he not suffered a torn ACL during his sophomore season with the Hoosiers — almost no one has been better at it than Anunoby, and coaches trust him to do it.

It's why the New York Knicks, with an eye toward winning their first NBA championship, traded two young players who had key roles on their playoff-caliber team — Immanuel Quickley and RJ Barrett — to the Raptors for Anunoby midway through 2023–24. They then signed Anunoby to a near-max contract in the offseason.

The difference he made was clear: In December, prior to acquiring Anunoby, the Knicks allowed a league-worst 123.6 points per 100 possessions. In January, with Anunoby in the lineup, they cut that mark to just 104.4 points per 100 possessions, the league's best. According to ESPN, it was the largest month-over-month turnaround on record.

Not surprisingly, wins and losses reflected Anunoby's impact. The Knicks went 27-5 in the 32 regular-season and playoff games that they played with Anunoby in the lineup and seemed poised for a deep playoff run before injuries — including a hamstring pull for Anunoby — saw the Knicks lose a seven-game series to the Indiana Pacers in the second round.

The data backs up the wins and losses: even while spending more time covering his opponents' most

OG Anunoby blocks a shot by Indiana Pacers forward Pascal Siakam in Game 1 of the Eastern Conference Finals on May 21, 2025.

dangerous offensive players than almost any other defender in the NBA, according to BBall Index, Anunoby was the league's sixth-ranked isolation defender, even while spending nearly as much time defending centers as point guards. Had injuries not limited Anunoby to 50 games in 2023–24, leaving him short of the required 65-game threshold, it's almost certain he would have been named to one of the NBA's All-Defensive teams, following up on the Second-Team nod he earned in 2022–23.

In 2024–25 it was more of the same as Anunoby ranked in the 95th percentile as a 1-on-1 defender while taking on the NBA's most difficult matchups and spending significant time guarding all five positions. He was eighth in the NBA in deflections per game (3.2) and seventh in total deflections (240), while setting a career-best mark for blocks (65) and finishing 11th in total steals, all while scoring a career-high 18 points per game and making a career-best 171 threes. He didn't make the All-Defensive Team — he finished 11th in the voting, missing by one spot — but that doesn't diminish his status as one of the league's best. Anunoby proved his worth during the Knicks' second-round upset of the defending champion Boston Celtics. The Knicks jumped out to a 2-0 series lead against Boston, with Anunoby helping hold Celtics star Jayson Tatum to 12-of-42 shooting, setting the stage for the Knicks winning the series in six games.

And what makes Anunoby that much more valuable is that he plays a critical role on offense as well. Since becoming a full-time starter in his third season, Anunoby was one of only three players — Paul George and Tyrese Haliburton were the others — to make at least 500 threes shooting 38 percent or better from distance while also averaging at least 1.5 steals.

"You can't say enough about what OG brings to our team," said then-Knicks head coach Tom Thibodeau shortly after Anunoby arrived in New York. "From steals to blocks, those plays are huge ... that activity is a talent [and] ... the impact he has on our team is enormous." ■

CAREER HIGHLIGHTS

- 2018–19 NBA Champion
- 2022–23 All-Defensive Second Team

5 Dyson DANIELS

POSITION PG, SG // **SHOOTS** RIGHT // **HEIGHT** 6'8" // **WEIGHT** 199 LBS // **DRAFTED** 2022, 8TH OVERALL

Michael Jordan, John Stockton, Gary Payton, Scottie Pippen, Allen Iverson, Rick Barry.

What do all of these players have in common?

In a single word? Greatness. They are all Hall of Famers with indisputable credentials. After they retired they were all enshrined as soon as they were eligible.

And while they are all different types of players, they share one common trait: the ability to create havoc defensively. It may not be the first thing that comes to mind, but they each had seasons — sometimes multiple seasons — when they counted 225 steals or more.

There are only 14 players in NBA history to have done it. In contrast 36 different players have averaged at least 30 points a game.

The steal is one of the most fundamental and unequivocal plays a defensive player can make. In one moment the opposing team has the ball and is trying to score, and in the next — frequently in the blink of an eye — the defender has it and is often in position to create an offensive chance for their own team.

They are big plays, and getting steals consistently requires athleticism, smarts and boldness.

During the 2024–25 season Dyson Daniels stole the ball 229 times, the most in a single season since Gary Payton had 231 steals in 1995–96, a gap of nearly 30 seasons. Daniels' work was done in 76 games and his 3 steals per game average made him one of just eight players to average at least that many steals per game while playing more than 60 games in a season and the first to do it since Nate McMillan in 1993–94.

Daniels is also the youngest to do it since data became available in 1973–74 and one of only two players to do it while playing less than 34 minutes a game. Alvin Robertson, who holds the NBA record for most steals in a season (301) and steals per game (3.7) and Seattle SuperSonics favorite Slick Watts are the others.

Dyson Daniels battles for the ball against Jalen Brunson of the New York Knicks in a game on February 12, 2025.

It perhaps shouldn't be all that surprising that Dyson has become one of the NBA's most respected defenders and noted ball hawks.

He grew up in Australia, the son of

Ricky Daniels, a former North Carolina State product who had a long and productive playing career in Australia. The young Daniels grew up a multi-sport athlete, starring in Australian rules football before giving it up to concentrate on basketball full time. It helps also that Daniels is 6-foot-8 with long arms, giving him an advantage while trying to strip balls from smaller point guards and unsuspecting centers alike. It's also why Daniels averages 0.7 blocked shots per game, too.

"I study the game, watch as much as possible every night to pick up on [a] player's tendencies," he said during his breakout season. "I'm trying to see where I can get the edge on people. If, as a defender, if you're reacting to what the offensive player is doing, you're going to be a step behind, so I'm always trying to find ways for how I can improve myself, create new chances to get steals, deflections, whatever. I'm a fan of the game, I study the game and do whatever I can to get the edge."

It didn't take long for Trae Young, Dyson's All-Star teammate, to grasp how impactful the young Atlanta Hawks guard could be.

"I see First-Team All-Defense as many times as he wants to be, as many years as he plays," the Hawks veteran point guard said. "You can just see what he's able to do now that he has the opportunity to play a lot ... defensively we're playing off of him."

This was during a stretch when Daniels had consecutive games of 4, 7, 6, 6 and 6 steals in the space of five games. The 29 steals he accumulated in the five-game period in November were notable because at that point no one else in the NBA had 25 steals for the season.

With the outsized performances came the high-end nicknames, among them "The Great Barrier Thief," given to him by his Hawks teammate Larry Nance Jr.

Daniels was drafted No. 8 overall in 2022 and took some time to find his feet in the NBA on a deep New Orleans Pelicans team. His breakthrough was helped when he was traded to Atlanta in the summer of 2024.

His offensive game also developed with the move, along with more opportunities, as Daniels averaged careers highs of 14.1 points, 5.9 rebounds and 4.4 assists with a career-best 53.6 effective field goal percentage.

And it isn't as if stealing the ball is his only defensive trick. In 2024–25 Dyson led the NBA in deflections per game (6.2) and total deflections — with his 443 being 169 more than second-place Keon Ellis and the most since the NBA began tracking deflections in 2015–16.

He was also a formidable on-ball defender as he ranked in the 99th percentile of BBall Index's matchup-difficulty measurement — indicating he spent almost all of his time defending the best players on other teams and was rated in the 100th percentile in his ability to guard 1-on-1 on the perimeter. It was no surprise when he earned All-Defensive First Team honors for his season's work.

Hawks coach Quin Snyder coached four-time Defensive Player of the Year Rudy Gobert in Utah, so he has experience with how an elite defender can affect the game. As one of the NBA's best paint-protecting bigs, Gobert plays a completely different style than Daniels, but Snyder appreciates the benefits all the same.

"Dyson is always wanting to and willing to take on the challenge [of guarding the other team's best player]," Snyder said after Daniels held Minnesota Timberwolves star Anthony Edwards to 7-of-20 shooting and forced him to turn over the ball five times in a game in which Daniels had 8 steals. "But I like what he did off the ball as well ... you don't take it for granted, but on some level there's an expectation there that he's going to do that because he does it so consistently."

CAREER HIGHLIGHTS

- 2024–25 Most Improved Player
- 2024–25 All-Defensive First Team

5 Luguentz DORT

POSITION SF, SG // **SHOOTS** RIGHT // **HEIGHT** 6'4" // **WEIGHT** 220 LBS // **DRAFTED** 2019, UNDRAFTED

It was a conversation between two elite basketball minds, LeBron James and JJ Redick, and the subject was defense. Specifically, it was what to do when a defender like Luguentz "Lu" Dort was going to be your matchup for the entirety of an NBA playoff series, when the stakes are higher, the physicality is ramped up and players of all stripes are looking to make a name for themselves.

Pause right there: That Dort and his unique brand of defense were being discussed by two of the NBA's biggest names should never go underappreciated given his unlikely journey to the NBA.

The Oklahoma City Thunder wing grew up in Montreal North and was raised by a single mother, a French-speaking Haitian immigrant.

"Montreal North's a tough neighborhood," Dort told the *Montreal Gazette* prior to his second NBA season. "Some of my friends went the wrong way. I felt like basketball basically saved me. Leaving my house early in the morning, coming back late at night, you couldn't really do anything [else]. I had to do this over and over the whole week."

He attended three different high schools in two countries and went undrafted after a single season of college basketball at Arizona State.

Dort showed an insatiable will to compete and excel, not to mention he had the physical dimensions of an NFL free safety. The Thunder recognized something in him and offered him a two-way contract and a chance to prove himself.

It didn't take long. Midway through his rookie season in 2019–20, Dort was signed to a four-year deal on the strength of his already stifling brand of defense and his potential to develop enough offensively to earn NBA minutes.

Dort first made a name for himself when OKC was matched up with the Houston Rockets in the first round of the 2019–20 playoffs when the NBA concluded the pandemic-interrupted season in the "bubble." His assignment was to make James Harden — who was at the end of a run where he finished second, first, second and third in MVP voting — miserable.

Dort succeeded as well as anyone else had at that stage, most notably holding Harden to just 18 points on 4-of-15 shooting in Game 7 of the Thunder's first-round series against the heavily favored Rockets, all while forcing Houston's primary ball handler into four turnovers. At the other end Dort went off for 30 points, setting a then-NBA record for most points scored by a 21-year-old in the seventh game of a playoff series. (Paolo Banchero surpassed this with a fiery Game 7 performance in the 2024 playoffs, in

which he scored 38 points against the Cleveland Cavaliers in a first-round series loss for the Orlando Magic.)

The Thunder lost the game and the series, so it was a bittersweet moment for Dort, but he had made his name and introduced basketball fans to the "Dorture Chamber" — the type of all-encompassing, never-pause defense that has become his trademark.

Through his first five seasons Dort had yet to earn recognition as an All-NBA defender, just missing out in 2023–24 when he finished 11th in the voting. But he got the recognition he long deserved when he was named to the All-Defensive First Team in 2024–25 as the focal point of the Thunder's No. 1–ranked defense.

"Honestly, I feel like the work I've been doing on that end of the floor has been the same for the past years," he said about the honor. "It's good that I finally got recognized for it. I give a lot of credit to my teammates and this whole team for the success that we've had. But I'm happy I got recognized for it."

Dort's offensive game has evolved as well, as he shot a career-best 41.2 percent from three in 2024–25 on a career-high 413 attempts — impressive progress given Dort shot just 30.7 percent from three in college. Dort's two-way game was on full display during the Thunder's run to the NBA Championship as he shot 44.7 percent from three while serving as the primary defender on the Pacers' star guard Tyrese Haliburton in the Finals.

But those who have had to play against him have long known what's what.

Which is how Dort's game became the subject of a conversation between James and Redick on their *Mind the Game* podcast, in which the NBA legend and his then-future Lakers coach broke down the minutiae of the sport at its highest levels. Redick asked James what it was like to go into a playoff series knowing that an elite defender — and Redick offered

Luguentz Dort defends as Jaylen Nowell of the New Orleans Pelicans tries to shoot in a November 13, 2024, game in Oklahoma City.

CAREER HIGHLIGHTS

- 2024–25 NBA Champion
- 2024–25 All-Defensive First Team

Dort as an example — had only one mission: to ruin his night.

"I think any time you go into a series with a defender that's capable of Lu Dort's skills, you can't have much FAT [which James defined as 'F-around Time'] on the court … I'm not coming out here trying to get in my bag," James said. "… It's if I'm in a pick-and-roll, you tell your big 'you've gotta screen him.' Yes, he's gonna try to fight through it, but I need you to screen him and get him off me for a little bit … If you play around with guys like that, they're gonna wear on you. They're gonna keep their body on you and make it physical."

Is there any higher praise than being top of mind as one of the NBA's best defenders when James is talking strategy?

The data backs up James' take. According to BBall Index, Dort was rated first in the perimeter isolation category and did that while spending more time on his opponent's primary ball handler than almost anyone else in the NBA, all while holding opponents to 47.9 percent on two-point attempts, which is 6.6 percent lower than the league average.

It all adds up.

"I've kind of watched him become a defensive stopper," said forward Dillon Brooks, an All-NBA defender and Dort's teammate on the Canadian national team. "Guys don't want to deal with that physicality all night — and what's crazy is that for his size, he's quick moving laterally, so he can stay in front and give guys hell the whole night by staying in front, making them take tough shots, midrange shots. I admire that and I admire his heart as well." ■

27 Rudy GOBERT

POSITION C // **SHOOTS** RIGHT // **HEIGHT** 7'1" // **WEIGHT** 258 LBS // **DRAFTED** 2013, 27TH OVERALL

There are two sides of the game, and Rudy Gobert has mastered one.

The Minnesota Timberwolves star center is an expert at preventing opposing teams from scoring. Sometimes he does it by rejecting shots left, right and center — the 7-foot-1 Frenchman, aptly nicknamed the "Stifle Tower," averaged 2.1 blocked shots per game through his first 12 seasons. More often he just forces other teams to miss shots that they would normally make: In 2023–24 Gobert held opponents to just 60.7 shooting from the restricted area, second-best among centers with at least 50 starts that season. In 2024–25 his opponents shot nearly 10 percent worse than the league average inside 6 feet, the fifth-best mark among players with at least 1,500 minutes of floor time. Perhaps most significantly, the mere presence of Gobert, lurking in the paint, encouraged players and even teams to try something different and usually outside of their comfort zone. Advantage Gobert.

"You want them to force guys into rushed decisions," Gobert told NBA.com as he was on his way to winning his record-tying fourth Defensive Player of the Year award in 2023–24. "But you've got to be OK with guys hitting tough shots. You've got to understand sometimes somebody's going to cross you up or sometimes you're going to get dunked on. But I'm going to be there. At the end of the day, it might look bad on one [clip] that goes viral, but [then there are] all the other clips you're not going to see of guys not even trying to shoot or guys getting blocked ... and that translates into winning."

Gobert's teams win. After being drafted 27th overall in 2013, it took a minute for the long-limbed project to adjust to the NBA game, but he was a regular for the Utah Jazz in his second season, a full-time starter in his third and was named to the All-Defensive First Team and a runner-up in DPOY voting in his fourth season, during which he also averaged 14 points, 12.8 rebounds, shot 66.1 percent from the floor and led the league in blocked shots. Not coincidentally the Jazz's win totals climbed from 25 to 51 over the course of those four seasons.

And the winning follows him wherever he goes. Between 2016–17 and 2024–25 Gobert's two teams, Utah and Minnesota, played at a 49-win pace and made the playoffs every year. He helped Minnesota to consecutive trips to the Western Conference Finals in 2024 and 2025. Over those years the Jazz and, later,

Rudy Gobert blocks a shot by Marcus Bagley of the Philadelphia 76ers on April 25, 2025.

CAREER HIGHLIGHTS

- 4-time Defensive Player of the Year
- 3-time All Star
- 2016–17 All-NBA Second Team
- 7-time All-Defensive First Team
- 2024–25 All-Defensive Second Team

the Timberwolves ranked on average sixth in team defensive rating. Four times his teams were third or better, and only once were outside the top 10.

It's his ability to serve as the focal point of a team's defense that prompted Minnesota to make a franchise-altering trade in the summer of 2022 to acquire Gobert from the rebuilding Jazz. The initial returns were mixed — the T-wolves won just 42 games in 2022–23, below their expectations, and four less than the previous season. But there were encouraging signs as the Timberwolves finished 10th in team defense — an improvement from 13th the season before — and still advanced to the playoffs despite a steady stream of injuries.

The 2023–24 season saw Minnesota win 56 games, the second-most in franchise history and the most in 20 years, and advance to the Western Conference Finals for just the second time, and the first since the 2003–04 season.

Gobert was at the heart of all of it as Minnesota posted the NBA's best defensive rating, allowing just 109 points per 100 possessions, more than 2 points per 100 possessions better than the second-best defensive team, the Orlando Magic — with the gap between first and second larger than the gap between second and 10th.

Not surprisingly Gobert was a runway winner as the NBA's Defensive Player of the Year for a fourth time, joining a list of four-time winners that includes only Dikembe Mutombo and Ben Wallace — both of them members of the Naismith Basketball Hall of Fame.

Minnesota was sixth in defense for 2024–25, and Gobert was named to the All-Defensive team for the eighth time in nine seasons.

"Rudy's driven the defensive culture here," said Timberwolves head coach Chris Finch during Minnesota's run to the conference finals in 2023–24. "It's a testament to his impact, his presence and what he's infused into this team on how important defense is and how great we can be when we play it."

For Gobert it's something that has come almost naturally. He has tremendous size and insight into the game and how offenses try to attack, which makes him an excellent communicator at the back of the defense — an underrated skill. He's also better at switching onto perimeter players than he sometimes gets credit for. During the 2023–24 playoffs Gobert held opponents to 6-of-21 shooting in switches. Overall opponents shot just 51 percent on all two-point attempts with Gobert guarding them, regardless of where on the floor, which is 3 percent better than the league average, according to NBA.com.

But perhaps Gobert's main attribute as a defender is how much he enjoys doing it, and how closely he identifies with the role.

"I've always loved it," he told NBA.com. "When I contest a shot and the guy misses, I get excited. You have to find joy in everything you do. It allows me to be happier. I just love winning." ■

GOLDEN STATE WARRIORS

23 Draymond GREEN

POSITION PF, SF // **SHOOTS** RIGHT // **HEIGHT** 6'6" // **WEIGHT** 230 LBS // **DRAFTED** 2012, 35TH OVERALL

Draymond Green rises up to block a shot by Minnesota Timberwolves' Naz Reid in Game 2 of the second round of the playoffs on May 8, 2025.

Draymond Green talks a lot. He has won four NBA championships, was named to the league's All-Defensive team nine times in 11 seasons beginning in 2014–15, won the Defensive Player of the Year award in 2016–17 and finished in the top three of the voting four other times, including in 2024–25 as a 34-year-old. He's an Olympic gold medalist and a future Hall of Famer.

But somehow Green is still known more for what comes out of his mouth than what he does on the basketball floor. Whether it's on his podcast or as part of the TNT broadcasts or when he simply decides to speak his mind to whichever microphone is handy, the words flow.

But that doesn't mean he's not worth listening to. Push past the bombast and there are few players in the NBA who are smarter, wiser or more willing to share their perspective.

Which is why his comments on the *Dubs Talk* podcast in March 2021 are worth paying attention to, because Green was talking about the two subjects he's most qualified to opine on: himself and defense.

His views: "I think when you look at the things that make a great defender: reaction time, toughness, being able to see the picture long before it develops, and most importantly, in order to finish a defensive possession, you've got to rebound. And I think I rebound well.

"And so when I look at all the facets that make up the defensive side of the ball, I think I'm great in every facet. So I think I'm the best defender to ever play in the NBA. I'll stand by that. I'll put myself up against anyone."

And you know what? He may be right. Certainly Bill Russell would have a word, as might Tim Duncan and prime Scottie Pippen. There are three men who have won the

CAREER HIGHLIGHTS

- 4-time NBA Champion (2014–15, 2016–17, 2017–18, 2021–22)
- 2016–17 Defensive Player of the Year
- 4-time All Star
- 5-time All-Defensive First Team
- 4-time All-Defensive Second Team

league's Defensive Player of the Year award four times — Ben Wallace, Dikembe Mutombo and Rudy Gobert — and none of them, you might notice, are Green.

But like opinions, awards are subjective. At the very least Green, since becoming a starter in his third season after being drafted 35th overall in 2012 as a senior out of Michigan State, has been among the very best defenders in the NBA for all the reasons he describes.

He's listed at 6-foot-6 but is comfortable guarding the league's biggest centers in the post, the most skilled ones on the perimeter and the most athletic ones rolling to the basket. He defends shots at the rim well but also has the determination to rotate to the perimeter to contest threes. He can stifle wings and turn away point guards. Most of all he knows what's coming before it happens, so some of his best defensive plays are executed before the offense can even get organized to use the set they were planning.

"He's a savant. He has an incredible defensive mind," long-time Warriors head coach Steve Kerr said of Green late in the 2023–24 season. "... From game-to-game, Draymond just has a good sense of what he needs to do to help us win ... A lot of games, he loves being the center fielder, just playing off the main guys so he can plug up gaps. It's just different from game-to-game."

Green is no one's favorite opponent, but he's earned their respect.

"He's good," the typically understated Nikola Jokic said of Green. "... He's playing physical. He's a really good defender. I think he can guard multiple positions. He's been doing that for a long time, so a really tough matchup for anybody in the league."

Green's contributions mean that the Warriors have been willing to put up with a long list of shenanigans the feisty veteran has gotten himself into, whether it's his multiple suspensions and altercations or his tendency to get into dustups with officials that has him among the league leaders in technical fouls every season. Green's role as the defensive conscience of one of the modern NBA's greatest teams has always earned him the benefit of the doubt.

Green showed in 2024–25 that even in his mid-30s he's capable of anchoring an elite defense. The ageing Warriors made a late run into the Western Conference playoff picture, finishing the season on a 20-7 rip after the All-Star break while posting league-best defensive numbers over the final third of the season. They followed that up by holding the No. 2–seed Houston Rockets to just 104 points per game, more than 10 points below their season average as the Warriors won the series in seven games before falling to the Minnesota Timberwolves in the second round.

Over his 11 years as one of the NBA best defensive players, Green has in some ways changed how great defenders are perceived, as he has done his best work with his mind and his well-honed sense of anticipation rather than by rising up and using otherworldly speed or athleticism to do the job.

Is he the greatest defender of all time? It's impossible to know, but if Green is talking, it's usually worth listening.

PORTLAND TRAIL BLAZERS

4 Jrue

HOLIDAY

POSITION PG, SG // **SHOOTS** RIGHT // **HEIGHT** 6'4" // **WEIGHT** 205 LBS // **DRAFTED** 2009, 17TH OVERALL

Sometimes you don't properly appreciate someone until they're gone.

Consider Jrue Holiday and the Milwaukee Bucks. With Giannis Antetokounmpo running roughshod over the NBA, the Bucks had emerged as a serious championship contender in 2018–19 and 2019–20, but they fell short of a title despite finishing with the Eastern Conference's best record and Antetokounmpo winning league MVP honors both years. A 60-win Milwaukee team lost in the Eastern Conference Finals in 2019, and a squad that played at a 62-win pace in the pandemic-shortened 2019–20 season was eliminated in the second round.

After two seasons of crushing disappointment, the Bucks decided to go all in and traded a king's ransom for Holiday, the widely respected point guard who was playing on a rebuilding team in New Orleans.

The payoff was immediate. Holiday was the stabilizing point-of-attack defender and sturdy locker room presence they needed, and in 2021 the Bucks broke through and won their first championship in 50 years, the signature play perhaps being when Holiday ripped the ball out of the hands of unsuspecting Suns guard Devin Booker, took it the other way and threw a pinpoint lob pass to Antetokounmpo to seal the win and the series in Game 6.

But after a couple more seasons during which the Bucks couldn't return to their championship peak, change was in the air again. Milwaukee decided the opportunity to acquire Hall of Fame–bound point guard Damian Lillard from Portland was too good to pass up, even if it cost them Holiday.

Holiday was in short order traded from a rebuilding Portland club to the Boston Celtics, another team trying to break through and win a championship after losing in either the Eastern Conference Finals or the NBA Finals five times in the previous seven seasons.

Once again, Holiday proved to be the missing championship piece as he helped Boston to a dominant 64-win regular season in 2023–24 and a 16-3 romp through the playoffs.

The Celtics, with Holiday as their primary defender on opposing wings and guards and someone who — at 6-foot-4 and 205 pounds — was rugged enough to hold his own when he got switched onto opposing big men, had the third-best defensive rating in the first season after Holiday arrived. Meanwhile the Bucks slid from fourth in 2022–23,

CAREER HIGHLIGHTS

- > 2-time NBA Champion (2020–21, 2023–24)
- > 2-time All Star
- > 3-time All-Defensive First Team
- > 3-time All-Defensive Second Team

Holiday's last season in Milwaukee, to 19th in 2023–24 — their first season without him.

The Celtics were a good defensive team before Holiday arrived, but it's telling that even on a team featuring some excellent perimeter defenders — Jaylen Brown, Derrick White and Jayson Tatum among them — it was Holiday who was trusted to guard opposing teams' most dangerous perimeter players most often.

Holiday emerging as the Celtics' primary perimeter defender was predictable to anyone paying attention.

"You know you put Jrue in any system, any coach is gonna ask him to guard the best player," said 6-foot-11 superstar Kevin Durant on the *Old Man and the Three* podcast. "I mean we played them 2018 second round [when Durant was in Brooklyn and Holiday with the Bucks], and he guarded me the whole series and picking me up full court, he was guarding me in the post. It was tough to dribble on Jrue Holiday. He slides his feet so well, he's got good hands, he's strong, he's got good instincts."

Durant's comments have been echoed by a cross section of the NBA's best guards and wings, with everyone from Stephen Curry to Lillard to Chris Paul singling out the Celtics star for his defense.

It's at the point now that some teams even alter their offense so that they don't have to try to score against Holiday more than necessary. For a defender, the ultimate compliment is when teams try to avoid you, like an NFL team might target the side of the field where the All-Pro cornerback isn't.

"I like being on the ball a lot, but it is like a sign of respect, though," Holiday told *The Athletic* in 2022. "Why go at him when you can go at somebody else?"

Luka Doncic might be one of the most dominant offensive players in the NBA right now, but every time he has to match up against Holiday, he knows he's going to be in for a tough night. In the 2024 NBA Finals, when Boston defeated Dallas in five games, Doncic did average 29 points and 5.5 assists, but his True Shooting percentage was just 53.0, whereas in the regular season Doncic averaged an NBA-leading 33.9 points a game to go along with 9.8 assists, with a career-best True Shooting mark of 61.7.

Doncic could have seen it coming. Back in 2022, when Holiday was still with the Bucks, Doncic was yet another league-leading guard to shake his head at the prospect of testing himself against Holiday. "Jrue is the best guard defender for me," said Doncic. "... it's very tough to go against him. I'm surprised he was never Defensive Player of the Year or something."

^ Jrue Holiday, playing for the Boston Celtics, defends as Josh Okogie of the Charlotte Hornets drives to the basket in an April 11, 2025, game in Boston.

Holiday missed out on his seventh career All-Defensive nod in 2024–25, but at age 34 and in his 16th season he has maintained his status as a defensive pillar, with Holiday routinely taking on the league's toughest defensive matchups (rated in the 94th percentile, according to BBall Index, and he earned an "A" or 90th percentile grade for his ability to suppress shots or make them difficult).

In a cost-cutting move during the 2025 offseason, the Celtics dealt their best defender back to the Portland Trail Blazers, which wanted to add Holiday's brand of championship-level defense to their up-and-coming roster. ■

13

Jaren JACKSON JR.

POSITION C, PF // **SHOOTS** RIGHT // **HEIGHT** 6'10" // **WEIGHT** 242 LBS // **DRAFTED** 2018, 4TH OVERALL

Playing elite defense in the NBA is typically something that players grow into. The speed of the league, the level of athleticism and skill, and the complexity of each team's offensive approach means that it can sometimes take years for younger players to have a positive impact on the defensive end of the floor.

But there are exceptions to that rule, and the Memphis Grizzlies' Jaren Jackson Jr. is most certainly one of them.

He was drafted 4th overall out of Michigan State in 2018, in part because of his potential as a defensive impact player. Athletes that are 6-foot-10 and 242 pounds and can comfortably guard wings and centers don't come along all that often.

He has the mentality for it, too, which helps.

"... I'll probably like slow down to let somebody shoot it just so I can block it," Jackson said of his defensive approach in college, where he earned Defensive Player of the Year honors in the Big 10, averaging 3.2 blocked shots a game in just 22 minutes of floor time. "... You know, it's demoralizing, because I'll try to like, you know, give them hope and try to take away at the same time. Blocking shots is just something I like to do."

It didn't take long for Jackson's potential to reveal itself at the professional level — he averaged 1.5 blocks and nearly a steal per game over his first three years in the NBA — but injuries and foul trouble limited his playing time, so it wasn't fully appreciated.

That changed in 2021–22, Jackson's fourth season, when the then-22-year-old led the NBA in blocked shots and averaged nearly a steal per game (while only playing 27.3 minutes per game) for a Memphis team that won 56 and advanced to the second round of the playoffs. He limited opponents to 41.7 percent shooting when he was the primary defender — or about 6 percent lower than the league average — ranking him second (behind Rudy Gobert at 41.6 percent) among NBA players with at least 900 contested shots.

Jackson was named to the All-Defensive First Team and earned perhaps the highest praise possible when Steve Kerr, head coach of the 2022 champion Golden State Warriors, said that Jackson's presence had required his battle-tested team to adjust in their hard-fought, second-round series win over the Grizzlies that preceded the Warriors' fourth title.

"The focus last year in the playoffs

Jaren Jackson Jr. blocks a shot by Cason Wallace of the Oklahoma City Thunder in Game 4 of the first round of the playoffs on April 26, 2025.

was not to try to challenge him at the rim going up on one foot and thinking you're gonna lay it up over him, because that's not going to happen," Kerr said of Jackson when the two teams met during the 2022–23 regular season. "So you've got to really attack the paint with the idea of keeping your feet on the ground, giving yourself options with a jump stop, moving the ball back out to the perimeter and forcing their defense to react. Otherwise, he's just loading up and you're having to score over the top of him."

And that's not easy.

The concerning part for the rest of the NBA was that Jackson was still improving.

In 2022–23 the Grizzlies won 51 games and finished second in the Western Conference. Jackson led the NBA in blocked shots again, this time averaging a career-best 3 blocked shots per game. He also averaged a steal per game, which was then his career best. Teams had a hard time scoring at the rim when he was on the floor, with opponents converting just 46.2 percent of their field goal attempts from inside 6 feet, which was 12.9 percent less than the league average on those shots. To drive the point home, when he missed the first 14 games of the season recovering from a broken foot, the Grizzlies had the 23rd-best team defense in the NBA, but after he returned from injury Memphis took off defensively and ended up with the second-best defensive rating for the season.

Jackson was named the NBA's Defensive Player of the Year, becoming just the second player — Dwight Howard was the other — to win the award at age 23 or younger. Jackson earned All-Defensive honors again in 2024–25, although Memphis struggled as a team, bowing out in the first round of the playoffs. The 25-year-old recorded 213 combined steals and blocks — seventh best in the NBA — and joined Shai Gilgeous-Alexander and Victor Wembanyama as the only ones to do it while averaging more than 20 points per game.

"Guys in this league are really talented. You just wanna make it hard on them. It's simple: I don't wanna get scored on, and I don't want our team to get scored on," he said. "... I really just want to win the game at all costs. I will do whatever. If that means putting me on a guard? Cool. If that means I have all these blocked shots? Cool."

What it means is that when Jackson is on the floor, your team's defense is almost certain to be running hot.

CAREER HIGHLIGHTS

- 2022–23 Defensive Player of the Year
- 2-time All Star
- 2-time All-Defensive First Team
- 2024–25 All-Defensive Second Team
- 2018–19 All-Rookie First Team

MINNESOTA TIMBERWOLVES

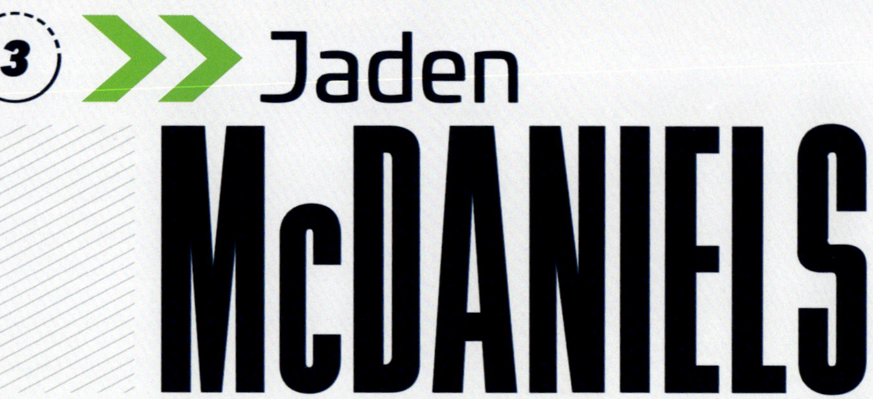

Jaden McDANIELS

POSITION PF, SF // **SHOOTS** RIGHT // **HEIGHT** 6'9" // **WEIGHT** 185 LBS // **DRAFTED** 2020, 28TH OVERALL

Anthony Edwards can be a bit of a jokester. The Minnesota Timberwolves guard is emerging as one of the faces of the NBA not only because of his dramatic athletic talent, but also because he seems to enjoy the job of being one of the best basketball players in the world.

So, it was reasonable that some might have thought Edwards was kidding at least a little bit when, during an interview at the 2023 NBA All-Star Game, he was asked about how the Timberwolves matched up against the Phoenix Suns, who had just acquired superstar Kevin Durant at the trade deadline to make them instant championship contenders, at least on paper.

"They got KD," Edwards said. "But we got Jaden McDaniels."

Edwards was dead serious, and in time the rest of the NBA came to understand why.

By the end of the 2022–23 season, McDaniels had proven himself to be one of the best defenders in the NBA, though perhaps his reputation hadn't quite grown past Minnesota.

But Edwards brought some attention to his teammate, and the data backed up the eye test on the slender 6-foot-9 wing who could seamlessly switch from defending point guards to power forwards.

McDaniels was the only player in the league that season to record at least 75 blocks and 70 steals. He led all wings in block rate, dropped opponents' expected shooting at the rim by 7 percent and spent more time guarding All-Star players than any defender in the league, all while appearing in 79 games.

When he wasn't named to an All-Defensive team at the end of the season, his teammates were dumbfounded.

"No Jaden is wild," said respected T-wolves point guard Mike Conley in a social media post.

Then-teammate Karl-Anthony Towns added, "Jaden McDaniels not making an All-Defensive team is criminal."

Making things worse was that McDaniels inadvertently broke his hand while punching a wall in frustration — he didn't realize there was concrete behind a curtain — and missed the Wolves' two play-in games and the first-round series against the Denver Nuggets.

The playoffs are where players get noticed, and McDaniels missed them.

"It was just hard to watch," said McDaniels after the season. "I'm a competitor, I love to play basketball. Sitting out at any time is kind of hard. It was a good experience to watch my teammates fight through the playoffs ...

[it] fuels me a lot. Getting motivation to get better every year and not want to miss an opportunity like that again."

A season later, in 2023–24, the Timberwolves forward got his chance to redeem himself.

He maintained his elite regular-season defense. According to BBall Index, McDaniels rated third in the NBA in both matchup difficulty and perimeter defensive rating, while helping establish Minnesota as the No. 1 defensive team in the NBA.

This time around McDaniels got his All-Defensive nod, earning Second-Team honors in his fourth season.

He even got a chance to prove his teammate Edwards right with his "we got Jaden McDaniels" comment when the Timberwolves matched up against Durant and the Phoenix Suns in the first round of the playoffs.

Minnesota swept the Suns in four games and McDaniels even got the last laugh offensively, as he helped hold Durant to just 18 points in Game 2 (nearly 10 points below Durant's season average) while scoring 25 himself on 10-of-17 shooting.

"ANT [Edwards] knows what he's talking about," McDaniels said afterward. "We all love to compete, so it was just something for me to have kind of a chip on my shoulder and myself knowing I still got to go out and play defense and guard KD and score as well."

For McDaniels it's proof that not every path to NBA success must be linear. He was a well-regarded prospect coming out of the Seattle-area high school scene. His older brother, Jalen McDaniels — who preceded Jaden to the NBA by one season — set the bar, and the younger McDaniels surpassed it, becoming a five-star recruit and being named a McDonald's All-American before playing one season at the University of Washington and going 28th overall in the 2020 draft.

It took a little bit of time for McDaniels to find his NBA niche, but by his third season he was excelling as one of the best defenders in the league and by his fourth season he was being recognized for it, earning both All-Defensive team recognition and a five-year, $136 million contract.

Those who have to deal with his combination of size, quickness, length and tenacity would look at that signing as good value.

Though McDaniels didn't make a repeat appearance on the 2024–25 All-Defensive team, his performance merited consideration as he was once again one of the focal points of an elite defense that made it to the Western Conference Finals. The Timberwolves were ranked 4th in defensive rating for the season, and according to BBall Index, McDaniels was in the 98th percentile as a 1-on-1 perimeter defender while taking on matchups that rated in the 99th percentile in difficulty. He was one of just two players to have at least 110 steals and 74 blocks for the season.

While the T-wolves don't yet have an NBA championship, they've got Jaden McDaniels, and with his exceptional defensive skills, they may have a fighting chance. ■

Jaden McDaniels blocks a shot by Golden State Warriors guard Brandin Podziemski in Game 4 of the second round of the playoffs on May 12, 2025.

CAREER HIGHLIGHTS

> 2023–24 All-Defensive Second Team

Ivica ZUBAC

POSITION C // **SHOOTS** RIGHT // **HEIGHT** 7'0" // **WEIGHT** 240 LBS // **DRAFTED** 2016, 32ND OVERALL

Ivica Zubac defends against Nikola Jokic of the Denver Nuggets in Game 2 of the first round of the playoffs on April 21, 2025.

When Ivica Zubac was growing up in a Croatian family in basketball-mad Bosnia and Herzegovina, he used to imagine himself playing in the NBA and maybe even for the Los Angeles Lakers.

It seemed a distant dream.

He was tall for his age, but otherwise unremarkable. He played club basketball in his small town and stayed up late to watch NBA games, getting hooked on the exploits of Kobe Bryant, Pau Gasol, Metta World Peace and Lamar Odom. One of his first basketball memories was watching Game 7 of the 2010 NBA Finals, when the Lakers toppled the Boston Celtics.

He continued growing and improving, eventually moving from home to play for a bigger club in Zagreb, the capital of Croatia. He began showing promise after growing 8 inches as a 15-year-old, but he was held back after suffering a stress fracture in his foot that cost him a season. Finally, age 17, things began to come together: He was playing for a first division professional club while still a teenager and an injury to another prospect gave him the chance to step in as a starter on the U19 Croatian national team. He was hard to miss as a 7-footer with good basketball IQ and a soft touch around the rim.

The young Zubac put his name into the draft and was taken 32nd overall by the Los Angeles Lakers in 2016, the same team he had stayed up late watching just four years before.

But Zubac's NBA journey was just beginning — his future in the league as unpredictable as his path to get there.

It took nearly a full decade in the NBA for Zubac to fully arrive as a star center, but it was with the other NBA team in Los Angeles, the Clippers, where he anchored one of the league's best defenses and earned recognition as one of the league's best all-around centers.

"He's grown into an elite big in this league. I don't think anybody saw it coming," Clippers teammate and 2018 MVP James Harden said of his pick-and-roll partner at the end of the 2024–25 season. "I don't even think he saw it coming, honestly, and

CAREER HIGHLIGHTS

> 2024–25 All-Defensive Second Team

he's only going to get better, that's the scary part."

Zubac's breakout was years in the making, but it was convincing when it arrived.

The nine-year veteran averaged career-best marks of 16.8 points, 12.6 rebounds and 2.7 assists while converting 62.8 percent of his shot attempts in 2024–25, compared to career averages of 9.2/7.4/1.2 on 61.2 percent shooting.

"The game is slowing down for me," Zubac said after posting 23 points, 18 rebounds and 6 assists in an early-season win over the Golden State Warriors. "I'm a lot more confident."

But perhaps the most significant benefit of Zubac's offensive uptick is that it drew more eyes to what he's been excelling at all along: establishing himself as one of the NBA's best interior defenders.

He's long been a problem for other teams in the paint. In every season, beginning in 2019–20, Zubac has been in the 91st percentile or better in deterring opponents' shots at the rim, with an average mark over five seasons of 96.5. It's a calculation comparing the number of opponents' shot attempts within 4 feet of the rim when a certain player is on the floor compared to when they are not. Given that shots at the rim remain the most valuable in basketball — even in the age of the three-pointer — having a center that discourages teams from even trying them inevitably enhances a team's overall defense. It helps, too, that Zubac has mastered being an intimidating paint presence without fouling. He was one of only three players in 2024–25 to play at least 2,000 minutes and accumulate at least 90 blocked shots while averaging 2.1 fouls per game or less.

But the Clippers wanted Zubac to aim even higher, particularly with their chances of contending for a championship as the aging Harden and the often-injured Kawhi Leonard run out of runway.

"[He should be] shooting for Defensive Player of the Year. I think he's that good, he can blitz. Sometimes, he can switch, he's good at deep drops, up to touch," Clippers head coach Tyronn Lue said prior to 2024–25. "I just think shooting for Defensive Player of the Year, I think that's his next step. Being one of the most elite defenders, he's already one of the top rim protectors, just continuing to take that next step."

Zubac took the message to heart and delivered his best season, on both sides of the ball, eventually earning himself All-Defensive Second Team honors.

"It's just reading the defense, being ahead of the play: [Who] is setting the pick, who has the ball, who has it going. Are we going to blitz, are in a deep drop?" Zubac said. "You have to be able to do multiple things and have multiple options on defense. You have to be able to adjust throughout your career, to whatever they throw at you, small ball, bigs in the post, shooting bigs, whatever it is."

For Zubac, the ability to make adjustments to what's happening around him has been the key to him making the transition from a small town in Croatia, where the NBA was a distant dream, to starring in Los Angeles as one of the NBA's best centers. ■

A GLOBAL GAME

When will an American basketball player win the NBA MVP award again?

Imagine floating that as a rhetorical question in 1965, 1975, 1985, 1995, 2005 or 2015?

It would be met with quizzical looks and likely ignored, if not ridiculed initially. Basketball is America's sport, invented locally (by a Canadian, but whatever), grown domestically and exported internationally. But for decades there was never any question that the best players in the world — and the NBA — were born in the land of Bill Russell, Wilt Chamberlain and Michael Jordan.

But in 2025? It's a perfectly reasonable question. When Oklahoma City star Shai Gilgeous-Alexander received the NBA's most prestigious individual award during the Western Conference Finals, it marked the seventh-straight year it had been earned by an international player.

It's just another example of how basketball's footprint has continued to expand and how what seemed like a distant dream has become a reality. In the late 1980s, visionaries like former FIBA secretary-general Borislav "Boris" Stankovic pushed the International Olympic Committee to allow the United States to include NBA players on its Olympic team. Former

Shai Gilgeous-Alexander accepts the award for Most Valuable Player on May 22, 2025. The 2025 award marked the seventh-straight year that a non-American had won the NBA's top honor.

NBA commissioner David Stern eventually signed off on it, introducing the world to the "Dream Team" for the 1992 Olympics and thus changing the sport in ways that still resonate more than 30 years later.

"The vision of Boris Stankovic started in 1987," Stern said years later, looking back on how the 1992 Olympics changed basketball forever. "He said there was simply no way the world would improve in basketball unless the NBA agreed to allow their players to play. We did and the payback is our sport is so much more global, and the competition is so much more intense."

It took time for the full effect to be felt.

For decades, leading up to the Dream Team, the ideal of competitive international basketball seemed like it involved every country other than the U.S., which forever stood above the crowd, untouchable by other nations. It was nice that basketball became popular in places as far-flung as China, Lithuania, Brazil and almost everywhere in between, but everyone knew that the U.S. was the world's leading basketball country.

But decade by decade, international teams got incrementally better against U.S. teams, eventually getting to the point where the lineups of seasoned international pros were too much for Team USA's squads of college-age players. It was initially shocking when Brazilian star Oscar Schmidt torched Team USA for 46 points as Brazil won gold at the 1987 Pan Am Games, handing the Americans their first international loss on home soil in their federation's history. It was even more shocking when David Robinson and a team of college stars were defeated in the semifinals of the 1988 Olympics. That was the first game the Americans had lost at the Olympics, save for the controversial loss to the USSR in the gold-medal final at the 1972 Olympics: After multiple clock malfunctions in the closing seconds — which the Americans were convinced were intentional — the Soviet Union got a last-ditch chance at the winning basket. Team USA refused to accept their silver medals after that match.

But all that it took for Team USA to reassert its dominance was to do what Stankovic was lobbying for and that Stern had convinced the NBA to rally around: send its best professionals to international competitions, beginning with the 1992 Dream Team going to the Olympics in Barcelona. Predictably, a lineup featuring 11 future Hall of Famers (and then-college star Christian Laettner) won the gold medal in a rout. Order was restored, and American teams won Olympic gold in 1992, 1996 and 2000. But that gap closed again as several top international programs raised their level and proved that even teams of NBA players — though perhaps not the *best* NBA players the U.S. had to offer — could be vulnerable. A team of NBA players finished a shocking sixth at the 2002 FIBA World Championship and settled for bronze at the 2004 Olympics and 2006 World Championship, making it three-straight global competitions in which Team USA didn't make the gold-medal game, let alone win it.

But again Team USA adjusted. They came up with the "Redeem Team" concept for the 2008 Olympics, where the NBA's best had to compete to make the team and USA Basketball committed to using the World Cup and other international events to test out rosters for the Olympics. The plan, masterminded by longtime NBA executive Jerry Colangelo, was an

From left to right, Karl Malone, John Stockton, Charles Barkley and Magic Johnson of Team USA's "Dream Team" celebrate winning the gold medal in men's basketball at the 1992 Olympic Games in Barcelona, Spain.

unequivocal success, with Team USA winning every Olympic gold from 2008 through 2024. But still, winning — or at least dominating — proved progressively more difficult.

The Americans lost in pool play to France at the 2020 Olympic Games in Tokyo and won by just 5 points in the gold-medal rematch. At the 2024 Olympics in Paris, Team USA was pushed to the limit in the semi-finals against Serbia and again in the gold-medal final by host France.

"We learned how hard these games are in the medal round, against the best teams," said Team USA head coach Steve Kerr. "... The game is global now. There's great talent all over the world."

Perhaps the best indication of that is the way the NBA has become an increasingly international league. At the start of the 2024–25 season, there were 125 players on NBA rosters born outside the United States, representing 43 countries. In 1991–92, the season prior to the Dream Team taking the Olympics by storm, there were 23 international players from 18 countries. Seven international players were selected as All Stars in 2025, the sixth-straight year at least five have been represented at the midseason NBA gala. But perhaps no development underscores the trend more than the way the MVP race has taken on the look of a UN meeting.

It took 38 years before a player born outside of the U.S. won the award — when Hakeem Olajuwon, the magnificent Nigerian center for the Houston Rockets, managed it in 1993–94. There was a blip in the mid-2000s when Canadian Steve Nash won consecutive MVPs in 2004–05 and 2005–06, followed by German star Dirk Nowitzki in 2006–07. But then it was 11 years of American players taking the NBA's top honor.

That run is most definitively over. When Gilgeous-Alexander — the pride of Hamilton, Ontario — became the second Canadian to be named MVP in recognition of his spectacular 2024–25 season, it served to not only maintain the streak of international players winning the award, dating back to Giannis Antetokounmpo winning the first of his two MVP awards in 2018–19, but also underline the overall dominance of international stars in the current era.

The 2025 voting was the fourth-straight year that there wasn't even an American in the top three. And looking ahead, the NBA's MVP ranks could retain an international flavor for years to come: Gilgeous-Alexander won his first award at age 26 and was born less than a year before Luka Doncic, the Slovenian national who had two top-five finishes in MVP voting and five consecutive All-NBA First Team nods on his résumé by age 25. Antetokounmpo, a Greek national of Nigerian descent, finished fourth or better in the voting for five-straight years after winning his two awards and was only 30 years old in 2024–25, when he finished third in the voting after completing one of the most prolific seasons of his career. Serbian star Nikola Jokic won the award in 2020–21, 2021–22 and 2023–24, was a runner-up in 2022–23 and had just turned 30 when he finished second to Gilgeous-Alexander in 2024–25. If Joel Embiid of Cameroon can recover fully from his offseason knee surgery in April 2025, he could resume the form that saw the Philadelphia 76ers star win the MVP award in 2022–23 and finish second the two years before.

There are plenty of brilliant American-born players in the NBA, but the ones who have been part of the MVP discussions in the past, or who have won the award, are all much closer to retirement than their primes.

The average age of the five most recent American MVP winners — James Harden, Russell Westbrook, Stephen Curry, Kevin Durant and LeBron James — was nearly 37 years old at the end of the 2024–25 season. The next most recent American to win the MVP award, Derrick Rose, retired after 2023–24. Before that you have to go to the late, great Kobe Bryant, who won the award in 2007–08 and retired from basketball in 2016 before dying in a tragic helicopter crash in 2020.

In the past few years, several American players have deserved consideration as potential MVP winners: Boston Celtics star Jayson Tatum has earned five All-NBA seasons — the last four First-Team honors — and won an NBA championship before his 27th birthday. Anthony Edwards has the electric talent and eye-catching stage presence that many MVPs have. A three-time All Star and two-time All-NBA player at just 23 years old, Edwards averaged a career-best 27.6 points a game in his fifth season, with his best basketball almost certainly still ahead of him. Both Jalen Brunson, who has emerged as one of the best clutch players in the NBA with the New York Knicks, or Donovan Mitchell of the Cleveland Cavaliers could merit consideration at some point.

But with the most recent cohort of American stars ageing out of their prime and the current group of international talent all in the heart of their peak, no one will be surprised if the international streak of MVP winners extends to eight years and beyond.

And that's without forecasting the number of MVP awards emerging San Antonio Spurs superstar Victor Wembanyama might end up claiming before his career is done. Almost invariably the MVP winner is selected from among a small handful of the NBA's best teams, so the Spurs — who last won a playoff round in 2017 and went six years without making the playoffs at all from 2019–20 through 2024–25 — have plenty of work to do on that end. But given that the French star has been

Victor Wembanyama with his Rookie of the Year trophy for the 2023–24 season. Wembanyama was the unanimous winner of the award, earning all 99 first-place votes.

Bakeer Fellah (No. 11) of Al Ahli Tripoli goes to the basket during the 2025 Basketball Africa League Playoffs on June 8, 2025, at SunBet Arena in Pretoria, Tshwane, South Africa. Al Ahli Tripoli defeated Kriol Star Basketball 107–81 and advanced to the Basketball Africa League (BAL) semifinals.

every inch — all 7 feet, 3 inches of them — the generational prospect he was projected to be when he was drafted first overall in 2023, it's easy to imagine San Antonio returning to prominence sooner than later. In that scenario Wembanyama — who certainly would have won Defensive Player of the Year in 2024–25 had his season not been cut short by a blood clot in his shoulder — would instantly be a perennial contender for the MVP award well before his 25th birthday in 2029.

Whatever their passport, it's safe to say the NBA's best are going to provide MVP voters with some difficult choices in the near future and beyond.

"All of us, we're going to get older. We're going to look at this age, and we're going to be like, 'amazing,'" Toronto Raptors head coach Darko Rajakovic, a Serbian national, said when he was hired for the 2023–24 season and his fellow countryman Jokic was on his way to his third MVP. "This era of the NBA is just amazing [with] the talent of all the players ... we're really blessed to live in this era and to be part of the NBA at this time. Just got to enjoy it and learn [from] those guys and how we can best continue to develop — the whole league."

But the international effect on the NBA could shape the game in ways we have yet to fully anticipate. Among the most significant developments was the announcement in March 2025 that the NBA is planning to launch a league under the NBA brand in Europe.

"Basketball is the No. 2 sport in Europe," NBA commissioner Adam Silver said in March 2025. He added that the league believed this was the "right time" to move forward with the idea. "It's widely popular. Hundreds of millions of fans. Roughly 15 percent of the players in the NBA right now are from Europe. Five out of the last six of our MVPs have been European. But there's a huge gap, I think, between the amount of interest in the sport and the development in terms of how we operate a league here in North America."

The plan is still in its early stages and won't involve the NBA having a division in Europe with teams that compete with the existing 30 North American teams. Instead it would be a standalone league in which top club teams from across Europe compete for their own championship.

In introducing the concept, Silver said the league would play by international rules, including 40-minute games, and would aim to retain the flavor of existing European leagues rather than being a facsimile of the NBA game as played in North America. The idea would feature a 16-team competition with 12 permanent clubs, drawing from some of the most storied basketball hubs in Europe — Madrid, Istanbul and Belgrade, for example — while tapping markets like Paris, London and Rome. It's not the first time the league has explored such a venture. In 2019 the NBA along with FIBA established an African-wide league, Basketball Africa League (BAL), where the best teams in the various domestic leagues qualified for BAL competition. This undertaking not only provided a new level of professional basketball for African players to aspire to but also helped build out the infrastructure for the sport in a region that already provides so many players to the NBA.

Establishing leagues in Africa and, soon, Europe in some ways represents a full-circle moment. The NBA's interest in expanding its global footprint dates back decades: In 1979 the Washington Bullets made a goodwill visit to China. From 1987 to 1997 the league hosted the McDonald's Open, a four-team round-robin tournament where an NBA team would play three top European clubs in various cities across Europe. In 2013 the league launched the NBA Global Games, a banner under which NBA teams hold training camps internationally and play exhibition and regular-season games.

The results have been evident for years now as the league's talent base has consistently been bolstered by the best from all over the world. It's something that might have seemed unlikely when basketball was being elevated by the likes of Magic Johnson from Michigan, Larry Bird from Indiana and Michael Jordan from North Carolina, but it appears inevitable now that many of the league's brightest stars come from Canada, Serbia, Greece and beyond. ■

RISING STARS

Amen Thompson

ORLANDO MAGIC

5 Paolo BANCHERO

POSITION PF // **SHOOTS** RIGHT // **HEIGHT** 6'10" // **WEIGHT** 250 LBS // **DRAFTED** 2022, 1ST OVERALL

For an NBA rookie, their "welcome to the NBA" moment is supposed to be a play or interaction when they realize that for all the time spent dreaming about playing in the world's most competitive basketball league, just getting there is no guarantee of future success.

It's a moment when they realize the players they idolized are even better than they thought, and that a lot of players they may not have thought about can make them look bad, too.

It can be humbling.

This was not Paolo Banchero's experience. The first overall pick by the Orlando Magic in the 2022 NBA Draft almost turned the idea upside-down. It wasn't the former Duke star from Seattle that got put on notice; it was Banchero letting the rest of the NBA know he had arrived.

Consider his first NBA game: October 19, 2022, against the Detroit Pistons. Early in the fourth quarter, the rookie power forward gets the ball on the left side of the floor just over half court and uses a couple of dribbles before gathering, rising and hurdling over veteran Pistons guard Cory Joseph for a jaw-dropping dunk. Joseph drops to the floor and everyone in the arena leaps to their feet.

Banchero finished his NBA debut with 27 points, 9 rebounds and 5 assists on 11-of-18 shooting. He didn't so much have a "welcome to the NBA" moment as he welcomed the NBA to his world for a moment.

He has rarely taken a backward step since. Banchero was a near-unanimous choice for the Rookie of the Year award in 2022–23 in recognition of a season that was both prolific and consistent: he scored 20 or more points 40 times, matching LeBron James' rookie year total.

Banchero's rookie averages of 20 points, 6.9 rebounds and 3.7 assists per game with a 46.5 effective field goal percentage (eFG%) compared favorably with other elite former Rookie of the Year winners, the likes of James (20.9 points, 5.5 rebounds, 5.9 assists and 43.8 eFG%), Kevin Durant (20.3 points and 45.1 eFG%), Luka Doncic (21.2 points, 7.8 rebounds, 6 assists and 49.7 eFG%) and Victor Wembanyama (21.4 points, 10.6 rebounds, 3.9 assists and 51.9 eFG%).

Banchero set a high bar for himself as the No. 1 pick but didn't seem to have any problem clearing it.

"I think I would say I met them [my expectations]," Banchero said at the end of his rookie year. "I wouldn't say I exceeded them. I think I did

everything that I wanted to do in my first year. It's definitely time to take it to another level in this next year. That's what I'm excited about."

Banchero is used to high expectations. His father, Mario Banchero, was a local football star in Seattle who went on to play tight end at the University of Washington, where he met Paolo's mother. She was one of the best basketball players in UW history, graduating as the all-time leading scorer before playing professionally, including a brief stint in the WNBA. She was a high school coach when Banchero was growing up, and he had little choice but to be immersed in the game.

"I wanted to be like her," Banchero said. "Knowing all the success she had, it inspired me from a young age."

By his second season Banchero was an All Star and the Magic were a 47-win playoff team in 2023–24. In Orlando's first-round series against the favored Cleveland Cavaliers, Banchero averaged 27 points, 8.6 rebounds and 4 assists while shooting 46.5 percent from the floor and 40 percent from three, some of which were improvements on his already impressive regular-season line of 22.6 points, 6.9 rebounds and 5.4 assists. The only other 21-year-olds to have a 22/6.5/5 season? James, Doncic and Michael Jordan.

That kind of production at that age makes people take notice. What they see is a 6-foot-10, 250-pound manchild who can both wiggle into tight spaces off the dribble like a point guard or bully his way into them like a linebacker, sending bodies flying and Banchero to the free-throw line: his 7.5 free-throw attempts a game since entering the NBA ranks Banchero third behind Joel Embiid and Shai Gilgeous-Alexander.

Banchero's third season was a frustrating one. He was off to an electric start, averaging 29 points, 8.8 rebounds and 6 assists — including

Paolo Banchero lays the ball up against the Washington Wizards on March 21, 2025.

notching a career-high 50 points in a win over Indiana — before he was sidelined for 35 games with a torn oblique muscle. It took him some time to return to form, and while Banchero's production improved for the third-straight season — he was one of six players to average at least 25 points, 7 rebounds and 4 assists for the year, the other five being either former MVPs or multiple All-NBA First Team selections — the Magic won just 41 games and were eliminated in the first round again.

But that doesn't change the outlook for Banchero, who in just three seasons established himself as a franchise player and a building block for years to come.

"There's a lot of talent that's under that 25," nine-time All-Star Paul George said on his podcast early in the 2024–25 season. "But [who do] I think who's shown that they're ready for that next jump and I think was a star? For sure, Paolo … he's a force." ■

CAREER HIGHLIGHTS

- 2022–23 Rookie of the Year
- 2024 All Star
- 2022–23 All-Rookie First Team

TORONTO RAPTORS

4 Scottie BARNES

POSITION PF, SG, SF // **SHOOTS** RIGHT // **HEIGHT** 6'7" // **WEIGHT** 227 LBS // **DRAFTED** 2021, 4TH OVERALL

Good to great.

It's not just the title of a best-selling management book on why some companies thrive and others fall back, it's the story of NBA stardom.

When you're picked fourth overall in the NBA Draft like Scottie Barnes was in 2021 by the Toronto Raptors, no one is looking for average. The hope — for both player and team — is that it is the start of a path toward excellence, lifting the fortunes of the individual and the organization alike.

The Raptors have certainly come to expect that of Barnes, the long-armed, broad-shouldered, multiskilled 6-foot-7 wing who can seemingly flip between playing point guard and playing center on the same possession, either offensively or defensively.

As the NBA's lone international franchise transitioned from its steady run as a championship contender, culminating with the 2019 title, to rebuilding for a new era, it is Barnes the Raptors have pinned the bulk of their hopes on.

"I think the most difficult thing to do when you do things like this is finding the Scottie Barneses of the world," then-Raptors president Masai Ujiri — twice recognized as the NBA's executive of the year — said after his young star's third season, when Barnes was named an NBA All Star for the first time. "And we're lucky to have a really good young player like this to build around."

With Barnes as the cornerstone, your construction project can take many different forms. Barnes can certainly score, but what makes him unique is the way he can do just about everything else at a high level, too.

Late in 2024–25, his fourth season with Toronto, Barnes displayed his versatility by joining multiple-MVP winners Nikola Jokic and Giannis Antetokounmpo as the only players since 2021–22 to accumulate at least 4,500 points, 2,000 rebounds, 1,300 assists, 200 blocks and 200 steals. The differentiating factor for Barnes is that he did all his work in the first four years of his career, while Jokic and Antetokounmpo were doing it in the heart of their Hall of Fame–worthy primes.

It's why Barnes' ceiling is so difficult to gauge, for certain. It's high, but how high, exactly?

Even as Barnes was putting the finishing touches on another box score–stuffing season — he averaged 19.3 points, 7.7 rebounds, 5.8 assists, 1.4 steals and 1 block — there remained some gaps. With his three-point shooting, for example, sliding from a career-best 34.1 percent in his third season to a career-worst 27.1 in season four, the 24-year-old's

ultimate ceiling is still in question. But if he can solve the shooting piece the answer will probably be something like, "superstar." As Kevin Durant said when Barnes was still a rookie, he has a lot of qualities that can't be taught: "I think a lot of young guys in the league have that competitive fire, but he has something a little extra as far as seeing the game a little slower.

"That's rare for a guy … how old is he? 19? 20? Sheesh! He not only plays the right way, but he's also only going to get better."

Barnes went on to win Rookie of the Year.

A few years later Durant and Barnes matched up, and it was the emerging star who got the best of the veteran legend in one late-season game. It wasn't just that Barnes contributed offensively, it's that he threw one of the NBA's all-time leading scorers completely off his game, holding Durant to just 5-of-15 shooting and 15 points, his second-lowest total of the season.

"I think I'm a high-level defender, one of the best defenders in this

Scottie Barnes drives the ball past the San Antonio Spurs' Keldon Johnson in an April 13, 2025, game.

league," Barnes said afterward. "I'm able to be able to guard multiple positions, switch, give the ball pressure because I move really well for my size and I'm out there reading things."

Barnes has a knack for elevating himself in big moments. He won gold medals for Team USA at the U17 and U19 World Cups. His high school team was undefeated in his senior season, and Barnes was voted freshman of the year in the Atlantic Coast Conference at Florida State. In his rookie NBA season, he showed a knack for putting up big numbers against marquee opponents: In home-and-away games against LeBron James and the Los Angeles Lakers, Barnes averaged 26 points, 13 rebounds and 5.5 assists. He averaged 20 points, 12 rebounds, 4 assists and 3 steals in his three meetings with Durant, and put up 25 points, 8 rebounds and 10 assists in a head-to-head matchup with

CAREER HIGHLIGHTS

- 2021–22 Rookie of the Year
- 2024 All Star
- 2021–22 All-Rookie First Team

then-two-time MVP Nikola Jokic in Denver. In his first playoff game he had 15 points, 10 rebounds and 8 assists before having to leave the game early when Philadelphia 76ers star Joel Embiid inadvertently stepped on his ankle.

Barnes zoomed way past "good" in his first NBA season, but through four seasons the question remains how far past it he will go. Those who work with him closely are betting he will go a long, long way.

"Scottie Barnes, he's such a humble, and down-to-earth kid," says Toronto Raptors head coach Darko Rajakovic. "But at the same time he has amazing ambition and wants to be really, really good. And he's back[ed] up all that with [a] great work ethic and coachability … He wants to be great." ■

2 Cade CUNNINGHAM

POSITION PG, SG // **SHOOTS** RIGHT // **HEIGHT** 6'6" // **WEIGHT** 220 LBS // **DRAFTED** 2021, 1ST OVERALL

Athletes like Cade Cunningham aren't used to failing. They have minimal exposure to it.

Their athletic experience is typically some version of this: set goal, work toward goal, reach goal, repeat.

It was always like that for the 6-foot-6 point guard from Texas. He was the star of one of the best high school teams ever at Montverde Academy in Florida, where he led a roster that featured six future NBA players to an undefeated season.

In one season at Oklahoma State, Cunningham averaged 20.1 points, 6.2 rebounds, 3.7 assists and 1.6 steals while shooting 40 percent from three and was a consensus First-Team All-American. And while the 2021 draft class was a deep one, there was never much doubt that Cunningham would go first overall.

But no one can completely escape adversity, certainly not in the NBA, and it was after reaching his lifelong dream that Cunningham had to deal with challenges he had never experienced before.

As a rookie the challenge was straightforward enough: the level of competition was higher than anything he'd encountered, and the rebuilding Detroit Pistons weren't very good. They went 23-59, losing more games in a season than Cunningham had in his entire high school and college careers combined.

And while Cunningham's statistics were promising for a rookie — he averaged 17.4 points, 5.5 rebounds, 5.6 assists and 1.2 steals, joining Michael Jordan, Magic Johnson and LeBron James as the only perimeter players to hit those benchmarks in their first seasons — he shot the ball poorly (41.6 percent from the floor) and turned it over too much (3.7 turnovers per game). He finished third in a very tight race for Rookie of the Year, the award going to his former high school teammate Scottie Barnes.

"Not winning Rookie of the Year was kind of devastating," his brother Cannen Cunningham said later in an interview with *The Ringer*. "... they'd lost a lot of games that year, and that was tough because he had never lost before in his life. But to still miss out on the award ... [It] shook him up a little bit."

The hard times were just getting started. Cunningham missed almost his entire second season after having surgery on his shin, as Detroit stumbled to a 17-65 season.

In 2023–24, things somehow got worse as Detroit lost 28-straight games, setting an NBA record for consecutive losses in a single season. Cunningham was on the floor and front-and-center for all of them.

"Everyday, I try to lead the squad," Cunningham said after the Pistons tied the record with their 27th-straight loss on their way to a franchise-worst 14-68 record. "I haven't been successful with that … everybody's trying to do everything they can to win games and be successful. I put a lot of that weight on myself, for sure."

But there were some glimmers of hope. Cunningham — in what was essentially his second season given he'd been limited to just 12 games in 2022–23 — averaged then-career-bests of 22.7 points and 7.5 assists while shooting 44.9 percent from the floor and 35.5 percent from three.

He also gained respect for how he handled the challenge of being the face of a team trying to find its way.

"We could not be more fortunate to have a guy like him here, leading the show," said Pistons head coach J.B. Bickerstaff, who took over the coaching reigns in Detroit for the 2024–25 season.

Dealing with and overcoming so many challenges in the first three seasons of his career finally paid off in his fourth season as Cunningham showed why any doubts anyone had about his ability to dominate at the NBA level were misplaced.

Cunningham had another breakout year, becoming just the sixth player in league history to average at least 26 points, 9 assists and 6 rebounds with an effective field goal percentage of 50.0 or better.

More importantly he did it while leading the 44-38 Pistons to their best regular-season record in nine years and their first playoff appearance in six. He was named an All Star for the first time and earned All-NBA Third Team honors after averaging 26.1 points, 9.1 rebounds and 6.1 assists for the season. He backed that up by helping the Pistons push the New York Knicks to six games in the first round of the playoffs, scoring 33 points and grabbing 12 rebounds in his playoff debut and averaging 25 points, 8.3 rebounds and 8.7 assists for the series, while also contributing 1.8 steals and 1.3 blocks per game

His goals remain commensurate with his talent.

"I'm not satisfied at all, I think there's still a lot more work to do," he said. "This city wants championships, and we're slowly building toward that."

After years of dealing with adversity and at times struggling as a pro, Cunningham was back to his old ways as a gifted player who had the ultimate answer for any basketball problem: his talent and his game.

Cade Cunningham rises to the rim during a February 12, 2025, game against the Chicago Bulls.

CAREER HIGHLIGHTS

- 2025 All Star
- 2024–24 All-NBA Third Team
- 2021–22 All-Rookie First Team

"I mean, you just got to get him the ball," Bickerstaff said after Cunningham hit a game-winner against Miami in late March 2025. "You try to get the ball in his hands, occupy the guys around him, and you know that Cade is going to be able to get his shot off … he's got the size, he's got the skill, you know he's going to get his look. We told him to go win the game, and he went and got it done." ■

0 Tyrese MAXEY

POSITION PG, SG // **SHOOTS** RIGHT // **HEIGHT** 6'2" // **WEIGHT** 200 LBS // **DRAFTED** 2020, 21ST OVERALL

Some players are destined for stardom, others have it thrust upon them.

As the 21st overall pick in the 2020 NBA Draft out of the University of Kentucky, you can make the case that Tyrese Maxey is in the latter group.

His first season with the Philadelphia 76ers tracked closely to what might be expected of a late first-round pick added to the roster of a team with championship aspirations: limited playing time and a restricted role when the on-court opportunities did present themselves.

The 6-foot-2 lightning bolt came off the bench — he made just eight starts and averaged 15.3 minutes per game. He averaged 8 points. There were signs of promise — he went off for 39 points, 7 rebounds, 6 assists and 2 steals in 43 minutes when the short-handed Sixers lost to Denver in January 2021 and had 30 points, 7 rebounds and 6 assists in a late-season win over Orlando — but those seemed like isolated blips. He finished 16th in Rookie of the Year voting and wasn't named First or Second Team All-Rookie.

The blips started popping up more closely together in season two, when Maxey — still only 21 years old — became a starter and averaged 17.5 points, 4.3 assists and 42.7 percent from three while playing alongside Joel Embiid and James Harden, two ball-dominant stars.

But he served notice that change was coming in the postseason. In the first playoff start of his career he flashed his electric potential again. He exploded for 38 points on 21 shots, including 5-of-8 from three, as he single-handedly overwhelmed the Toronto Raptors, a team that featured Fred VanVleet and Kyle Lowry, a pair of guards with All Stars on their résumés and who were just two seasons removed from leading the Raptors to an NBA title. Maxey followed up with 23 points, 9 rebounds and 8 assists on 8-of-11 shooting in Game 2. The Sixers won the series in six games as Maxey averaged 21 points a game on 50/40/90 shooting splits.

"It's a testimony to the work," Maxey said after his Game 1 breakout. "I always tell people the work that you put in when nobody else is around, early mornings, 6 a.m., late nights, it shows when you perform in front of thousands."

But Maxey's biggest test was yet to come. After another step up in his third season — his scoring jumped again, this time to 20.3 points a game while maintaining his efficiency (43.4 percent from three) for a 54-win Sixers team that lost in seven games to the Boston Celtics in the second round of the

CAREER HIGHLIGHTS

> 2023–24 Most Improved Player

> 2024 All Star

playoffs — his fourth season presented an entirely new challenge.

Harden, the Sixers co-star along with Embiid, forced a trade out of Philadelphia on the eve of the 2023–24 season. Overnight Maxey went from a solid third banana with upside to the second-most important player and lead guard on a team hoping to win a championship and best leverage Embiid's prime.

Maxey had his believers, but this was a new role with new demands and a new level of scrutiny.

No problem. Maxey helped Philadelphia jump out to an 8-1 record with a string of performances that just seemed to get better and better. Without having to share responsibilities with another guard, it seemed like Maxey was unleashed, combining his blurring speed with his deep shooting range and drawing comparisons to Damian Lillard, who had ridden that mix to a spot on the NBA's 75th anniversary team. It all came together on November 12, 2023, when Maxey scored a then-career-high 50 points in a win over Indiana. He added games of 51 and 52 points later that year, joining Joel Embiid, Allen Iverson and Wilt Chamberlain as the only Sixers to have three or more 50-point games in the same season.

"He just wants to get better," Embiid said of his teammate afterward. "He wants to learn. He's willing to learn; he listens. Extremely humble. I've always said he's the hardest-working person I've ever been around, and that's saying something. He doesn't take plays off. He always finds a way to get better. Obviously he's doing great, but I think he has an even brighter future. I think he can get to another level.

"Philadelphia's got a good one. He's

Tyrese Maxey shoots over Aaron Nesmith of the Indiana Pacers in a game on January 18, 2025, in Indianapolis.

going to be here for a long time, and like I said, he's The Franchise."

Maxey finished the regular season with new career highs in points (25.9), assists (6.2), rebounds (3.7), three-pointers (3), steals (1), blocks (0.5) and minutes (37.5) per game. Despite being elevated into the full-time point guard role Maxey averaged a miniscule 1.7 turnovers per game, too. He was named an All Star for the first time as he earned league-wide recognition with the NBA's Most Improved Player award.

It hasn't been all smooth sailing. The Sixers were eliminated by the New York Knicks in six games in the first round of the 2024 playoffs — though not before Maxey set a playoff career-high with a 47-point, 9-assist performance in Game 5, with Philadelphia facing elimination — and the 2024–25 season was a major disappointment. Embiid missed most of the season due to injury and Paul George, the high-profile free agent acquisition Philadelphia made in the offseason, badly underperformed before his season was also cut short by injury. Maxey was limited to a career-low 52 games in part due to a season-ending finger injury, and the Sixers missed the playoffs for the first time in eight years.

Under more pressure and with less support than at any point in his career, Maxey increased his scoring average for the fifth-straight season (26.3 points per game), and at age 25 emerged as the Sixers' brightest star for the future. ■

CLEVELAND CAVALIERS

4 Evan MOBLEY

POSITION PF // **SHOOTS** RIGHT // **HEIGHT** 6'11" // **WEIGHT** 215 LBS // **DRAFTED** 2021, 3RD OVERALL

A successful NBA player comes in a wider variety of shapes and sizes than most would think, at least at first glance.

Sure, "tall" is the first attribute that comes to mind, but it's far from the only one that matters. Chris Paul is one of the best point guards — and best players — of all-time, but he's barely 6 feet and looks more like a high school running back than an NBA star. Nikola Jokic — arguably the best player on the planet — is certainly tall enough, but outside of that everything about his physical appearance screams ordinary.

But it's hard to argue with the right combination of height, wingspan and mobility. Throw in a good dose of basketball IQ and you have the ingredients of a superstar.

Evan Mobley defends against Myles Turner of the Indiana Pacers in Game 4 of the second round of the playoffs on May 11, 2025.

Which brings us to Evan Mobley, the Cleveland Cavaliers big man who is simultaneously one of the best players in the NBA and a young athlete who seems to have barely touched the depths of his potential.

Mobley has all the attributes of NBA greatness: he stands 6-foot-11, has a 7-foot-4 wingspan and runs the floor easily. Though he's a little on the thin side, his height, reach and mobility make up for that.

Add in that he uses his gifts intelligently and diligently (on defense especially), and it is no surprise he was taken third overall in the 2021 draft by the Cavs after one season at the University of Southern California, or that he was the runner-up to Scottie Barnes for NBA Rookie of the Year, or that he was named to the All-Defensive First Team in his second year, or that he was voted an All Star midway through his fourth season. Adding to the All-Star nod, he earned All-NBA Second Team honors and recognition as the NBA's Defensive Player of the Year in 2024–25.

Quite literally, Mobley was built for this. It's why Hall of Famer, NBA champion and former MVP Kevin Garnett tagged the Cavs star as the current NBA player who he sees the most of himself in.

"Evan Mobley … when I watch him, he spaces up. He attacks the rim. He uses his left hand more than me. Evan Mobley is long, he blocks shots, he's effective at the post," Garnett said during a public appearance at the NBA

CAREER HIGHLIGHTS

- > 2024–25 Defensive Player of the Year
- > 2025 All Star
- > 2024–25 All-NBA Second Team
- > 2024–25 All-Defensive First Team
- > 2021–22 All-Rookie First Team

Abu Dhabi Games prior to the 2024–25 season. "He can hit from 15 or 17 feet. I'm more energetic and passionate than him ... but Evan Mobley is the future."

There was no argument from Mobley: "That's a great compliment from a great player," Mobley said when asked about Garnett's comments. "I definitely look up to him, watched a lot of his games, and definitely [incorporated] a lot of [his] game into mine, so I love to hear that."

But for all his success — Mobley averaged a career-best 18.5 points in 2024–25 and joined Kevin Durant as the only players in NBA history to average at least 1.1 made threes per game and 1.5 blocked shots with a True Shooting percentage of 64 or better — it's Mobley's upside that remains most intriguing.

He showed signs of what his ceiling could be during the 2023–24 playoffs against the eventual NBA champion Boston Celtics. The Cavaliers were missing All-Star center Jarrett Allen for the entire series and leading scorer Donovan Mitchell for the last two games of the five-game set. But Mobley responded to the increased demands placed on him as he averaged 21.4 points, 9.4 rebounds and 3.2 assists on 62.7 percent shooting for the series, including going off for 33 points and 4 assists on 15-of-24 shooting while facing elimination.

It's a process, however. The NBA's very best players are typically elite scorers and operate with extreme confidence. Mobley is still growing into those expectations.

"I've said this to Evan — your next step is believing you have all of the tools," Cavaliers head coach Kenny Atkinson said as Mobley helped Cleveland to the second-best regular season record in franchise history at 64-18. "There's a belief with these guys ... they just have this almost irrational confidence ... Evan is not a not-confident person, but we need to get him to be a little more irrational. A little more, 'Man, I'm going to be this guy.' I think that's his next step. All the tools are there."

Mobley's calling card has always been his defense. For him to reach his ceiling, his offensive game will need to expand to match his defensive gifts, and his determination to impact both ends of the floor will need to grow accordingly.

The signs are there, however. Along with winning his first Defensive Player of the Year award in 2024–25, Mobley set a new career mark for effective field goal percentage (64.4) and made more threes (85) in his fourth season than he did in his first three seasons combined, all while playing just 30 minutes a game.

The Cavaliers' season didn't end the way they had hoped as they were upset in the second round by the Indiana Pacers, but Mobley set career postseason marks for points (17.1) and effective field goal percentage (66.7).

Success breeds confidence, and Mobley is starting to feel it like the star he was built to be.

"Yeah. I'm definitely starting to feel like [a star]," he said at the 2025 All-Star Game. "All the hard work is definitely paying off. I've been in the gym these past few years trying to work on my offensive game. Keeping my defensive game the same level and I feel all the hard work is definitely paying off now." ■

28 Alperen SENGUN

POSITION C // **SHOOTS** RIGHT // **HEIGHT** 6'11" // **WEIGHT** 235 LBS // **DRAFTED** 2021, 16TH OVERALL

With the amount of attention young players get in the age of YouTube highlights and endless social media posts and boasts, it's far more likely for a rising basketball prospect to be over-hyped and unable to deliver than the opposite.

Falling through the cracks or not being properly evaluated heading into the NBA Draft almost seems impossible.

But it happens. Most famously, Nikola Jokic — arguably the best player in all of basketball today — was the 41st overall pick in the 2014 draft, with television coverage of the moment the Denver Nuggets selected him missing because the network cut to a Taco Bell commercial.

In the case of Alperen Sengun, the oversight wasn't quite as dramatic — the Turkish teenager was taken 16th overall by the Houston Rockets, smack in the middle of the first round — but there were voices leading up to the draft arguing that he should be taken much higher than he was projected or was finally chosen.

The argument was simple: Sengun was dominating one the best professional leagues in Europe as an 18-year-old.

Former Memphis Grizzlies executive and NBA columnist for *The Athletic* John Hollinger made the point plainly in one of his draft preview columns, writing midway through Sengun's season with Besiktas J.K. in the Turkish League:

"He is second in the league in scoring, rebounding and blocks. Nobody has had a PER [player efficiency rating] above 30 in this league for the last decade ... Sengun's is at a stratospheric 32.9, which needless to say leads the league by a wide margin. Did I mention he's 18?

"If he fails with this kind of track record in a good overseas league, he'll be the first of his kind."

But — as with Jokic, who went on to be MVP of the Adriatic League the year after he was taken by the Nuggets and the year before he made his NBA debut — there were naysayers. At 6-foot-11, Sengun wasn't particularly tall for a center and he wasn't a high-flying athlete. There were questions about his shooting and whether he would defend well enough to be helpful given the speed at which NBA games are played.

The concerns were significant enough that no one wanted to use a high lottery pick on Sengun, although Hollinger pegged him as the fourth-best player available in what was a talented 2021 draft class. But when he was available at pick No. 16, the Rockets, who had already selected Jalen Green second overall, took the leap.

Alperen Sengun dunks the ball in a game against the Philadelphia 76ers on March 17, 2025.

CAREER HIGHLIGHTS

> 2025 All Star

Lucky them. If the 2021 draft were to be held again with the benefit of four NBA seasons worth of knowledge, Sengun would be taken no worse than fourth overall, with only Cade Cunningham (originally taken first overall by Detroit), Evan Mobley (third by Cleveland) and Scottie Barnes (fourth by Toronto) having strong cases to still go ahead of him. There's an equally strong case that Sengun should go first. Among his draft class Sengun ranks fifth in total points scored, second in total rebounds, fourth in assists and second in field goal percentage among those who have played at least 200 games.

No less an authority than Jokic saw early on what Sengun could bring.

"I think he's really talented," Jokic said of Sengun squaring off against him in the Turkish big man's second season. "Maybe this is going to sound weird, but I think they need to play a little bit more through him. Sometimes they look a little bit more stagnant with all their threes. The guy has the talent. He can pass the ball, he can post up, he has the touch around the rim. You can see some different moves that he's made."

For his part, Sengun — who has drawn comparisons to the Nuggets' star because of their shared European heritage, endless toolbox of post moves and court vision — has said, "It makes me happy when they compare me to him because he is my idol."

The Rockets hired a new coach, Ime Udoka, for the 2023–24 season and brought some veterans to help turn around the franchise after two losing campaigns in which Sengun was a peripheral part of the offense. Given a more prominent role and a better supporting cast in his third season, Sengun broke out, posting season averages of 21.1 points, 9.3 rebounds, 5 assists and 1.2 steals on 53.7 percent shooting, becoming the only player ever to have achieved those thresholds in their age-21 season or in any of their first three NBA seasons.

Meanwhile the Rockets improved to 41 wins after having just 17 wins the year before Sengun was drafted.

In 2024–25, he followed up by posting 19.1 points, 10.3 rebounds and 4.9 assists on 49.6 percent shooting and was named to his first All-Star team as the Rockets won 52 games and finished second in the Western Conference before losing to the Golden State Warriors in the first round of the playoffs.

No one is underrating Sengun anymore.

"He's so skilled," his veteran teammate Fred VanVleet said to ESPN.com during Sengun's breakout third season. "He's unguardable. He's got a thousand moves. He's learning the higher aspects of the game now that he's going to be a featured guy and probably be an All Star ... He's going to keep learning the steps to [be one of] the greats, and what they got to deal with every night. But yeah, he's a problem."

Especially for the teams that had a chance to draft him but didn't. ■

HOUSTON ROCKETS

1

Amen THOMPSON

POSITION SF // **SHOOTS** RIGHT // **HEIGHT** 6'7" // **WEIGHT** 209 LBS // **DRAFTED** 2023, 4TH OVERALL

You have to see it to believe it.

The stories of Amen Thompson's athleticism preceded him: his blinding speed, impossible jumping ability and combination of quickness, power and grace that seems to have been borrowed from the domain of the big cats — lion, tiger, panther, take your pick.

When Amen and his equally mesmerizing twin brother, Ausar Thompson, were playing and training with Overtime Elite, an Atlanta-based professional development league for 16- to 20-year-olds, stories of them wowing overseas professional teams by being bigger (they stand 6-foot-7), faster and stronger were common currency during the pre-draft process.

But the NBA is a different beast. When Amen Thompson was taken fourth overall by the Houston Rockets (Ausar went one pick later to Detroit), there was a wait-and-see component regarding how or if his singular talent would transfer. The NBA is perpetually stocked with athletic marvels. Talent alone guarantees nothing, and Thompson's question mark as a perimeter shooter certainly invited a degree of skepticism.

But most of those doubts melted away after Thompson averaged 9.5 points, 6.6 rebounds, 2.6 assists and 1.3 steals while playing just 22 minutes a game, which was enough to earn him a spot on the All-Rookie team in 2023–24. Sure, his shooting was suspect (13.8 percent from three and 68.4 percent from the free throw line) and it wasn't clear if he had a specific positional profile, but the kid could do things other NBA players simply couldn't.

"One of a kind, bro," Rockets big man Steven Adams said of Thompson via the *Houston Chronicle* midway through the 2024–25 season, Thompson's second year. "I haven't played with anybody like this. His speed is just like, unbelievable. And then just his second jump, first jump, is so quick off the ground, it's crazy. I actually haven't seen that type of athleticism, to be honest."

To be clear, Adams played with Russell Westbrook for six seasons, including 2016–17, when the then-Oklahoma City Thunder star won the NBA MVP award, and with Memphis Grizzlies star Ja Morant for two seasons, so he knows what it's like to see teammates move like they've been shot from a cannon or have access to a trampoline.

In his second season Thompson was the same version of himself, just better, as he averaged 14.1 points, 8.2 rebounds, 3.8 assists, 1.4 steals and 1.3 blocks on 55.7 percent shooting. But

what all his kinetic gifts meant took clearer form as the Rockets began winning more games. The jump from 22 wins the season before Thompson was drafted to 41 in his rookie year was easily attributable to a range of factors: a new coaching staff, the Rockets adding some quality veterans to supplement their young core and the improvement of those younger players — Jalen Green, Alperen Sengun and Jabari Smith Jr., among others.

But when the Rockets took another jump in 2024–25 to 52 wins and a spot in the Western Conference playoffs, it was hard not to overlook Thompson's contributions. The box score numbers were just a small part of it.

It turns out having a 6-foot-7 defender, who is significantly more mobile and explosive than almost anyone in the league, that the Rockets can deploy to cover everyone (he has shown himself capable of guarding all five positions) or no one (Thompson roaming freely to make plays is a nightmare for opponents) contributes to winning.

For the season the Rockets had 10 five-man lineup combinations that were at least 5 points per 100 possessions better than the opposition and Thompson featured in eight of them. He was the only player in the NBA to average at least 1.4 steals and 1.3 blocks per game, and he subsequently earned the first of what will likely be many All-Defensive team honors. He received First-Team recognition in just his second season as he helped the surprising Rockets to the second seed in the Western Conference, though they eventually lost in the first round to the Golden State Warriors. Though Thompson worked hard in 2024–25 to increase his stat line from his rookie numbers, he took the most pride in being disruptive defensively.

"When they call me up for a screen and the [opposing] guy's like, 'Get out, get out, we don't want him on the switch,' that feels good," Thompson said in an interview with *The Athletic*. "I'm not going to lie, it feels good."

Amen Thompson rises up for a slam dunk in a March 23, 2025, game against the Denver Nuggets.

CAREER HIGHLIGHTS

- 2024–25 All-Defensive First Team
- 2023–24 All-Rookie Second Team

All the positives add up. As great as Victor Wembanyama has been since being taken first overall by the San Antonio Spurs in the 2023 draft, it is Thompson, not the Spurs star, who leads their draft class in WinShares. And while the Rockets are one of the NBA's most exciting young teams for many reasons, Thompson's rise as a game-changing-level star has undoubtedly raised their ceiling.

There is plenty of growing to do as a shooter and a decision-maker with the ball, and he still needs to define his role — is he a future point guard? The NBA's smallest yet fastest and most explosive small-ball center? It almost doesn't matter given the plays Thompson is able to make when the other team has the ball or when his team has it and he can roam freely in transition or in the half court.

Through his first two seasons it's clear that Thompson will figure out how to maximize his rare gifts to the benefit of the Rockets and their fans, and at the expense of the rest of the NBA. ■

ORLANDO MAGIC

22 Franz WAGNER

POSITION SF // **SHOOTS** RIGHT // **HEIGHT** 6'10" // **WEIGHT** 225 LBS // **DRAFTED** 2021, 8TH OVERALL

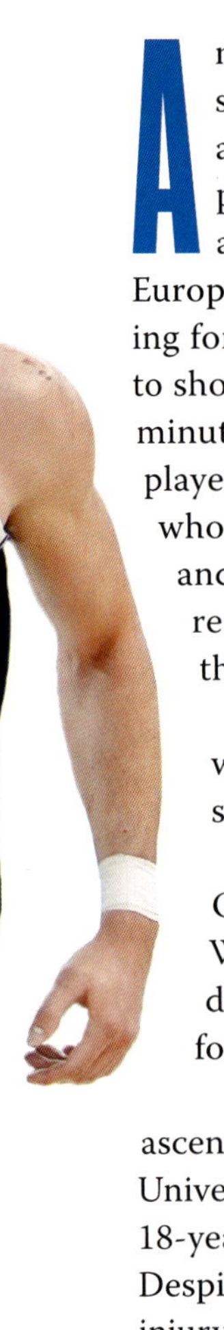

An NBA player's destiny is often shaped by opportunity. There are plenty of superb college players who never get drafted and many pros striving in Europe or the G-league simply waiting for a crack they can squeeze into to show that they're worthy of NBA minutes. And there are enough NBA players on the fringes of a rotation who are good enough to be starters and role players and handle bigger responsibilities if they could get the chance to take them on.

It's true even for budding stars who have been labeled a cornerstone piece for a young team.

Consider the situation Orlando Magic star Franz Wagner found himself in during the early stages of his fourth season.

Wagner's star had only been ascending since he arrived at the University of Michigan as a skinny 18-year-old from Berlin, Germany. Despite an early-season wrist injury he was named to the Big 10 All-Freshman Team and then was named Second-Team All-Big 10 as a sophomore. But given he stood 6-foot-10 and could handle the ball and create for others, NBA teams saw lots of potential. It was no surprise that the Magic took him with the eighth overall pick in 2021.

And in his first three years in the NBA, his trajectory continued to trend up: he was selected for the All-Rookie First Team and in year two finished second among sophomores in points (18.6), fourth in assists (3.5), fourth in steals (1), sixth in rebounds (4.1) and fourth in WinShares for a rebuilding Magic team.

Season three showed more progress, as the Magic won 47 games and qualified for the playoffs, forcing the heavily favored Cleveland Cavaliers to a seventh game before bowing out in the first round, with Wagner setting career marks in points (19.7), rebounds (5.3) and assists (3.7).

The Magic had big expectations for 2024–25 on the strength of their previous season, but a lot of it was predicated on Wagner's teammate Paolo Banchero — the No. 1 pick in the 2023 draft — making the leap to stardom.

But things changed when Banchero tore his oblique muscle on his right side five games into the year and missed the next 35 games.

It was just the opportunity Wagner needed. Over a 20-game stretch before Wagner went down with his own oblique injury, the 23-year-old averaged 26.1 points, 6 rebounds and 6.3 assists as the Magic — who were missing several other key rotation players due to injury in what ended up being a snake-bitten season — went 13-7.

"I think I had a little adjustment period. I think it's a little mentality shift for me as well. The way I grew up playing was a lot of off the ball and just taking really good shots all the time. I think sometimes it's okay to take a mid-range shot and stuff like that." Wagner told NBA.com. "That's something that's not ingrained necessarily or wasn't taught to me from a young age. So, it's a good challenge for me. I say this all the time: it's just super cool to get these opportunities and I want to make the most of them."

While a 20-game sample is hardly definitive, Wagner had already shown signs of his ability to lift a team as he led Germany to its first-ever gold at the 2023 FIBA Basketball World Cup. And it is worth noting that the only players to go 26/6/6 over the entire 2024–25 season were Nikola Jokic, Giannis Antetokounmpo, Luka Doncic, Jayson Tatum and Cade Cunningham. The first four have five MVPs and 21 All-NBA First Team nods among them, while Cunningham made the All-NBA Third Team for the first time in 2024–25.

It wasn't just Wagner's scoring and playmaking that stood out.

"I thought he was incredible," Magic head coach Jamahl Mosley said after Wagner contributed 18 points, 7 rebounds and 5 assists while playing lockdown defense on Damian Lillard down the stretch of a crucial late-season road win over the Milwaukee Bucks. "I think the way in which he takes on that challenge, guarding some of the team's best players and not backing down, and then being asked to do the task on the offensive end as well. You can't say enough about what he does."

The numbers say a lot though.

Over the course of the 2024–25 season, the fourth-year forward became just the seventh 23-or-younger player in league history to tally at least 5,000 points, 1,300 rebounds and 1,000 assists during their first four NBA seasons, something he managed to do in just 277 career games, with only LeBron James, Doncic, Anthony Edwards, Russell Westbrook, Chris Paul and Jokic doing it in a shorter period of time.

Franz Wagner shoots over two Cleveland Cavaliers defenders in a game on February 10, 2025, in Orlando.

Wagner led the Magic — who finished second in overall defensive rating — in defensive estimated plus-minus (EPM), according to DunksandThrees.com, and was ranked 14th league-wide.

CAREER HIGHLIGHTS

> 2021–22 All-Rookie First Team

Were it not for his own oblique injury that cost him 21 games mid-season, Wagner would have almost certainly been an All Star for the first time and in strong contention for an All-NBA nod.

It turns out that Wagner may be the rarest of NBA gems — a high scoring, playmaking, two-way star who can carry a team. He just needed the opportunity. ■

SAN ANTONIO SPURS

Victor WEMBANYAMA

POSITION C, PF // **SHOOTS** RIGHT // **HEIGHT** 7'3" // **WEIGHT** 235 LBS // **DRAFTED** 2023, 1ST OVERALL

There are no limits.

That's what the basketball world has learned about Victor Wembanyama in his all too brief NBA career.

What we do know is already impressive. Like LeBron James and perhaps almost no one else in NBA history, the 7-foot-3 French teenager arrived in the league with expectations that were almost unfair in their scope — the No. 1 pick would be the best rookie in his class, sure, but would he be an All Star? Would he end up being a generational talent? — and then he went on to exceed them.

There were questions about how his long, slender frame would manage the ruggedness of NBA competition, or whether his multifaceted skill set would translate offensively, or if the defensive dominance he demonstrated at lower levels of competition would be as meaningful against the best players in the world.

Wembanyama answered all these questions.

His rookie NBA season was one for the ages as he averaged 21.4 points, 10.6 rebounds and 3.6 blocked shots a game, tops among his draft class in each of those categories. He also averaged 3.9 assists per game, connected on nearly 2 (1.8) threes per game and snatched 1.2 steals. He did it while playing a conservatively managed 29.7 minutes a game over 71 starts, as the San Antonio Spurs wanted to build him up to NBA loads carefully.

Even so Wembanyama finished his rookie season as the first player of any level of experience to score 1,500 points (1,522), block 250 shots (254) and hit 100 three-pointers (128) in a single season, and he was the first rookie since Shaquille O'Neal in 1992–93 to average at least 21 points, 10 rebounds and 3 blocks per game.

Victor Wembanyama blocks the shot of Charlotte Hornets center Moussa Diabate in a February 7, 2025, game.

It was no wonder Wembanyama became just the sixth player in league history to win Rookie of the Year honors by unanimous vote.

"My goals were always to help my team as best as I could and get better as the year went on," Wembanyama said after the award was announced.

"I knew in order to do this I had to be individually good on the court and dominant."

But as remarkable as his statistical profile shows him to be, it's the in-person Wembanyama experience that reveals how high his ceiling is as he trends toward becoming a truly transformational player

In the early parts of his rookie season opponents would venture into the paint or the restricted area near the basket and try to score like they routinely have so many times in their careers only to have shot attempts swatted away by Wembanyama like a counselor playing a camper at summer camp. Later there was the spectacle of players driving toward the rim, catching a glimpse of Wembanyama closing in with his 8-foot wingspan and then electing to not even take a shot — the ultimate form of deterrence.

"Just super unique," said Knicks forward OG Anunoby, himself one of the NBA's most respected defenders, after playing Wembanyama for the first time. "Never seen anyone that tall in my life. So yeah, he's just really tall. Covers a lot of ground. He changes the game."

When Wembanyama was on the floor as a rookie, the rebuilding Spurs' defensive rating was 111.4 per 100 possessions, good for the NBA's fifth-best defensive mark, but when he sat San Antonio gave up 119.8 per 100, the league's worst. It's that discrepancy along with his prolific shot blocking — he is the only player other than Manute Bol to have a blocked shot percentage of 10 percent — that saw the budding French star finish second in voting for the NBA's Defensive Player of the Year award, with fellow Frenchman Rudy Gobert winning the voting for a record-tying fourth time.

Wembanyama's response? "It [was] deserved," he said of Gobert's win. "Because after that it is no longer his turn."

Wembanyama's ambition is one of his most valuable traits because his talent matches his goals. After helping France to a silver medal at the 2024 Olympics, Wembanyama wasn't satisfied that France had pushed the star-laden, gold medal–winning Americans to the limit.

"I'm learning, and I'm worried for the opponents in the next couple of years," he told the *San Antonio Express-News* in the aftermath of the gold-medal game. When asked if he meant FIBA opponents or the NBA, Wembanyama said "Everywhere."

In his second season he was well on his way to delivering against his own sky-high expectations. He averaged more points (24.3 per game), grabbed more rebounds (11) and blocked more shots (3.8) and became just the second player in league history to average at least 10 rebounds and 3 made threes (3.1) per game. He also recorded his first 50-point game on November 13, 2024, in a 139–130 victory over the Washington Wizards. He was named an All Star and was expected to earn All-NBA honors and his first of what will likely be several Defensive Player of the Year awards when news hit that shocked the NBA: Wembanyama's second season would be cut short in February after he was diagnosed with a blood clot in his right shoulder. It's a concerning condition, career-ending in some cases, like for NBA Hall of Famer Chris Bosh. But with treatment it has shown to be manageable, and indications are Wembanyama's career won't be affected permanently.

Basketball fans can only hope the Spurs' star has the long-term health outlook that matches his vast potential. ■

CAREER HIGHLIGHTS

- 2023–24 Rookie of the Year
- 2025 All Star
- 2023–24 All-Defensive First Team

OKLAHOMA CITY THUNDER

8 Jalen WILLIAMS

POSITION SG, PF // **SHOOTS** RIGHT // **HEIGHT** 6'6" // **WEIGHT** 220 LBS // **DRAFTED** 2022, 12TH OVERALL

Jalen Williams was always good. He was just small.

That is the simplest explanation for how a player who had to play three seasons at a mid-major college could be an All Star and a key cog on one of the best teams in the NBA just a few short years later.

Had Williams grown to 6-foot-6 before he left high school in Arizona, he might have been able to catch on at a more prominent school than Santa Clara, which has a strong basketball tradition (two-time MVP Steve Nash played there) but is a long way from one of the typical powerhouses that attract future NBA lottery picks.

He might have had a more prominent role sooner at college, too — he averaged just 7.7 points a game as a freshman. It also didn't help that his sophomore year was curtailed by the pandemic, limiting practice time and trimming Santa Clara's schedule to just 18 games.

But things eventually came together. The growth spurt that saw him sprout 5 inches from his sophomore year of high school to freshman year of college meant he eventually had the perfect measurements for an elite NBA wing: 6-foot-6 with a 7-foot-2 wingspan. The guard skills he emphasized before he grew gave him shooting and ball-handling abilities that would transfer well at higher levels of competition. That he had to play three years in college rather than one or two meant he had another year or so to showcase how it was all coming together.

Williams' slow but steady progress was rewarded on draft night when the Oklahoma City Thunder looked at his junior season, in which he averaged 18.5 points, 4.4 rebounds, 4.2 assists and 1.2 steals while shooting 51.4 percent from the floor and 39.6 percent from three, and made him the 12th overall pick in the 2022 NBA Draft.

Williams has kept it coming as a late bloomer whose story is nowhere close to being completed. He finished second in the Rookie of the Year voting as the Thunder jumped from 24 wins the season before he arrived to 40 wins in 2022–23. By his second season in the NBA he was a starter and an emerging star on a 57-win team that earned the first seed in the Western Conference, and he was just one of four players to average at least 19 points, 4 rebounds, 4 assists and a steal while converting better than 40 percent of this three-point attempts, joining a list that included LeBron James, Kyrie Irving and Jimmy Butler.

"Special," four-time NBA champion Draymond Green said of Williams during his breakout second season.

"Dude can shoot, he can pass, he can handle, he can finish, he can defend. He has great size, so he can guard multiple positions. He's athletic. He's great in the pick-and-roll. Like … Jalen Williams is special. Over/under two years until he's an All Star himself. I'm going to take the under. He is a problem."

Green was wise to take the under. Williams was an All Star in season three and earned All-NBA Third Team honors as well. The Thunder had the best record in the Western Conference, and Williams was a big reason why. As his superstar teammate Shai Gilgeous-Alexander put it, "You don't have this record because of one good player … You have to have a second All Star to help. When I'm out of the game he's carrying the load. Averaging 20 a game on hyper-efficiency and we're first in the west."

Williams averaged 21.6 points, 5.3 rebounds, 5.1 assists and 1.6 steals during his third season, making him one of just four players to average at least 21/5/5 and 1.5 steals for the season.

But it was Williams' defensive contributions that may have told a bigger story about his ultimate ceiling.

Long-term injuries to the Thunder's two 7-footers, Chet Holmgren and Isaiah Hartenstein, and their back-up big man, Jaylin Williams, meant for a five-game stretch in the first half of 2024–25 the Thunder had no choice but to play "small" — without a traditional big man.

But someone still had to take jump balls and someone still had to guard the other team's center, so for the Thunder, that someone became Williams, who joined the Cleveland Cavaliers' Evan Mobley as the only players in the NBA to earn both All-NBA and All-Defensive recognition in 2024–25.

"I just tried to make [guarding big men] a skill, add something else to my game," Williams said. "I feel like I do damn near everything well on the court. So in my mind, it was just one of those things. Like, why wouldn't I be able to do it? And I just kinda keep getting the opportunity to do it."

Jalen Williams shoots over Grayson Allen of the Phoenix Suns in a game on April 9, 2025, in Phoenix.

Willams added more signature moments during the Thunder's run to the 2024–25 Championship, including going off for 34 points in a pivotal Game 4 win over the Minnesota Timberwolves in the Western Conference Finals and 40 points in a crucial win over the Indiana Pacers in Game 5 of the Finals. For the seven-game series Williams averaged 23.6 points, 5 rebounds and 3.7 assists while drawing comparison to a young Scottie Pippen for his ability to impact games defensively.

CAREER HIGHLIGHTS

- 2025 All Star
- 2024–25 All-NBA Third Team
- 2024–25 All-Defensive Second Team
- 2022–23 All-Rookie First Team

It all added to Williams' growing reputation as one of the most valuable types of players in the modern NBA: a two-way wing who can spread the floor with his shooting, drive to the paint with force, create plays for others along the way and defend multiple positions, sometimes all of them.

All Williams needed to grow into his potential, it turned out, was to grow. ■

THREES 3.0

Go down shooting.

The Boston Celtics' defense of their 2024 NBA championship didn't go as planned. Despite a 61-win season and the No. 2 seed in the Eastern Conference, Boston's 2024–25 season ended in a six-game second-round loss to the New York Knicks. Making things worse, Celtics star Jayson Tatum suffered what ended up being a torn Achilles tendon in Game 4, putting the team's 2025–26 season in jeopardy.

During the playoffs there were many ups and downs for the storied franchise, but one thing remained constant: Boston was going to shoot a lot of threes, and if they missed a lot? Shoot some more.

Celtics head coach Joe Mazzulla assessed the outcome of Game 1 of the second-round series — a 108–105 loss to the Knicks in overtime in which Boston *missed* 45 threes while putting up 60 of their 97 shots from behind the three-point line — and shrugged.

There were no demands to drive the lane harder or get the ball inside more or chase down the misses with more aggression.

"I look at the process and the shot quality, [and] our shot quality was high," said Mazzulla, who made putting up as many threes as possible part of the Celtics' identity after he took over the head coaching role in 2022–23. "There were probably eight to 10 shots that [we] could be better at for sure."

The Celtics kept putting them up, hoisting 40 threes in Game 2 and making just 10 as they lost and fell behind 0-2 in the series. They had now missed a staggering 75 three-point attempts in two games. Facing a must-win situation in Game 3 on the road at Madison Square Garden, their commitment to the three-ball saved them — at least temporarily — as they connected on 20 of their 40 attempts in a blowout win.

The Celtics may have seen their chance at becoming the NBA's first repeat champion since the Golden State Warriors unravel in the second round, but they went down on their own terms. They averaged 46.2 three-point attempts for the six-game series, an NBA record for any playoff series but, remarkably, still shy of the record 48.2 per game Boston got up during the 2024–25 regular season.

In some corners, people might have been happy to see the Celtics stumble — and not just fans of the Los Angeles Lakers, their traditional rival. The explosion in three-point shooting, with the Celtics' record-setting embrace of it a significant element of their 2024 championship, has raised alarms: was the three-ball overtaking a game built on passing, cutting, defense and dunks? The NBA's old-guard, represented by *Inside the NBA*'s Charles Barkley, Kenny Smith and Shaquille O'Neal, made themselves heard while discussing a game in late December 2024 in which the Celtics and the Chicago Bulls combined for 108 three-point attempts and missed 75 of them. "It's a copycat league," Barkley said, incredulous that shooting more threes than twos was the tactic teams were copying.

Games with a high volume of threes aren't so bad when teams are making shots, but when the inevitable misses pile up, it can be hard to watch.

The pace of change has been hard to keep up with. The 1986 NBA champion Celtics — one of the best teams in league history, which relied on the talents of Larry Bird, one of the league's most lethal shooters — attempted just 34 three-pointers across six games in their Finals win over the Houston Rockets that year. A more telling stat: the 1985–86 Celtics took 393 triples for the season, compared to the 3,955 the 2024–25 Celtics hoisted, a 10-fold increase. Forty years later the game is almost unrecognizable in that respect.

The reason for the change is

Jayson Tatum of the Boston Celtics gestures after scoring a three-pointer in Game 3 of the Eastern Conference Semifinals versus the New York Knicks on May 10, 2025. The Celtics won 115–93 as they recovered their three-point stroke and gained a crucial road win.

fairly straightforward: shooting and, more importantly, making threes are conducive to winning. If the Warriors' four championships with Stephen Curry as the fulcrum weren't enough proof, the Celtics winning the 2024 championship while putting up 41.5 threes per game in the Finals should be the clincher. Copycat league or not, the Warriors' and Celtics' success made it seem essential for any team with championship aspirations to shoot threes well, and to do this they would need to take more of them than teams ever have before.

It's not that threes being a big part of the game is a new thing, it's just that they've never been bigger. If you thought the "three-point revolution" began 20 years ago in the early days of Steve Nash and the "Seven Seconds or Less" Phoenix Suns and culminated a decade later with the Warriors' dynasty years, think again. We're at "Threes 3.0."

The real question is if we've reached "Peak Three" or if there is more to come. The (likely) last championship of the Warriors' dynasty came in 2021–22 and that team — the last of the Stephen Curry–Klay Thompson "Splash Brothers" era — set a then-Finals record for three-point shots attempted per game at 41.8 in a six-game series win over the Boston Celtics. That series the Warriors took 40 more threes over the course of the Finals than Boston did.

When Jayson Tatum, Jaylen Brown and the Celtics returned to the Finals in 2024 against the Dallas Mavericks, they took their experience in losing the 2022 Finals to heart and launched the aforementioned 41.5 threes per game — 11 more per game than the Mavs did in the series — and won the franchise's NBA-record 18th title in five games.

On the other hand, in 2025 the Oklahoma City Thunder proved that copious amounts of threes are not the only way to win a championship. The Thunder won the title by turning back the clock at least little bit as they defeated the Indiana Pacers in seven games while averaging just 29.4 three-point attempts per game in the Finals. Then again, though the Thunder had a record-setting defense to rely on, they knew they needed to get more threes up. After squeaking out a series-shifting win in Game 4 while shooting just 3-of-16 from deep, Thunder head coach Mark Daigneault called their approach "unsustainable." In Game 5 Oklahoma City shot 14-of-32 from three — their best result of the series — and changed the course of the Finals.

The three-point revolution took some time.

Even Steve Kerr, the head coach of the Warriors, the team most closely associated with ushering in the era of the three, wishes he was quicker on the uptake. Before becoming head coach of the Warriors prior to the 2014–15 season, Kerr had been general manager of the Phoenix Suns from 2007 to 2010.

Looking back, he regrets that he didn't do his part to help speed along the evolution sooner. It was Mike D'Antoni — with Nash as his on-court muse — who first preached and popularized a three-point focused offense. When they were putting up 25 threes a game, the league average was 16. For context, in relative terms it would be like a team suddenly averaging nearly 60 threes in today's game. The Suns' embrace of the deep ball turned out to be remarkably successful as Phoenix averaged 58 wins per season in D'Antoni and Nash's four years together in Phoenix.

But for various reasons — injuries, bad calls and bad luck, mostly — the D'Antoni Suns couldn't get over the hump. Their run in the upper reaches of the Western Conference topped out with a pair of trips to the conference finals in 2005 and 2006. Under Kerr the Suns moved away from D'Antoni's preachings, even going so far as trading for an aging Shaquille O'Neal to get more size, even if it meant being slower and congesting the paint. Eventually, after one more playoff frustration, D'Antoni resigned at the end of the 2007–08 season. After largely unsuccessful stints with the New York Knicks and Los Angeles Lakers, D'Antoni caught on with the Houston Rockets in 2016 and recommitted to his "three-point first" strategy, pushing the boundaries even further. Between 2016–17 and 2019–20, the Houston Rockets averaged 54 wins and set new marks for three-point frequency every season, in many ways setting the stage for where the Celtics are now.

"I was there in Phoenix as GM, and I have that same regret [about not shooting more threes]," Kerr said in early 2025 with the benefit of 15 years of hindsight. "What Mike was doing was really cutting edge, but there was a lot of thinking then like, 'We can't win that way.' And so I was part of everybody [else] at that at the moment where it's like, 'Is this the right thing to do?' You don't really know. So I have the same regrets, and looking back, I'm like, 'Shit, Mike was on to it.' I wish I had encouraged him and said, 'No, no, keep going.' But I didn't. I was part of the traditional thinking, you win with the defense and can't shoot too many threes, all that stuff."

Coaching the Warriors, Kerr had his greatest successes leaning heavily on the three-point prowess of Curry and Thompson, the best shooting duo in NBA history. He has no qualms

»
Steve Nash of the Phoenix Suns shoots a crucial three-point shot to send Game 6 of the Western Conference Semifinals against the Dallas Mavericks into overtime on May 20, 2005. The Suns won the game 130–126 and the series 4-2.

NASH
13

about how those teams approached the game but recognizes that — if anything — he didn't lean on Curry and Thompson's three-point shooting enough.

"The reality is everything in this game evolves," Kerr continued. "When [D'Antoni and Nash] were with the Suns [in 2004–05] and they were taking 25 threes a game, everyone was going crazy, like, 'I can't believe this is happening.' Our theory that first year [with the Warriors] was to have Steph and Klay to shoot as many threes as possible. We didn't necessarily want other people shooting threes that year because we didn't have a ton of shooting and spacing otherwise ... but what's happening now in Boston, that couldn't have happened over night. That had to happen over time as the game evolves."

What started out as what many perceived as a gimmick has in a relatively short period of time become basketball orthodoxy. The three-point line was introduced by the old American Basketball Association (ABA) in 1967 but wasn't adopted by the NBA until the 1979–80 season. It barely mattered, teams almost never shot three-pointers. In the 1980 NBA Finals between the Lakers and the Philadelphia 76ers, the two teams combined to shoot just 20 threes in the six-game series, making just one. The use of the shot grew incrementally until the Suns made it a primary part of their offense. Two decades after D'Antoni and Nash, the 2024–25 league average was 37.6 three-point attempts per game. That average would have been a record number for a team right up until the Rockets put up 40.3 per game in D'Antoni's first season there in 2016–17. In 2024–25, inspired by the Celtics' example, seven teams averaged 40 threes per game (if you round up slightly) and 12 took 38 or more. Nothing like that has ever happened before.

There are concerns, similar to those voiced by Barkley, O'Neal and Smith. As more and more teams shoot more and more threes, some feel that NBA offenses have become stale or cookie cutter: spread the floor, drive the lane, kick the ball out, swing it one or two times, put up a three and repeat — a reflection of an analytically-based style of play in which open threes and layups have proven to be the most efficient way to score. The flipside is that all the concerns are "much ado about not much," with the biggest change being that more teams are taking fewer long two-point shots and instead are taking a step or two behind the line before putting it up. Meanwhile the added court spacing has allowed for more drives and dunks.

From the athletes' perspectives, adaptation to the three-game is key — especially for established players who've seen the changes happening over the course of their careers. In 2025 Kyrie Irving was just 33 years old, but the Dallas Mavericks star spans generations, at least when it comes to three-point shooting. He's always been able to pull it — he's a career 39.5 per game shooter from beyond the arc — but early on, even as the No. 1–overall pick out of Duke and a player who has never lacked confidence, he was relatively measured in his volume. He was a two-time All Star before he even cracked five attempts a game for the first time in 2014–15. In his 14th season in 2024–25, he got up to 7.2 attempts per game with a peak of 8.3 in 2022–23.

"I enjoy the freedom. There are rumblings that people aren't happy with the NBA game because of all the threes but as a player, I enjoy the freedom," Irving said in December 2024. "It's been a bit of an adjustment for myself ... [but] the NBA game is very fast, we're getting up and down, and there's not as many foul calls, so there's more opportunities for the ball

to go up. And when you're an efficient shooter, and you're working on your game, I think you should have that confidence to go out there and let it fly.

"But I think we're seeing a lot of systems be designed around shooting threes, a lot of threes, 50 threes, 60 threes. And I mean, we played against a team like that [Boston] in the finals [in 2024], where we had to watch them launch shots, and if they make 45 percent of them, and they shoot, you know, 60 of them, it's still a

Kyrie Irving, then of the Brooklyn Nets, shoots a three over MarJon Beauchamp of the Milwaukee Bucks during a December 23, 2022, game in New York. That season, Irving averaged a career high 8.3 attempts per game and made 37.9 percent of them.

decently good number. So we've had to adjust while also being aware of maximizing our own skill sets."

It's a similar story from Damian Lillard, who is third behind Curry and Los Angeles Clippers star James Harden in three-point attempts among active players. Lillard shot 6.1 threes a game in his Rookie-of-the-Year season with the Portland Trail Blazers in 2012–13 and had nearly doubled that total — to a career-high 11.3 per game — a decade later in his last season with Portland, before joining the Milwaukee Bucks.

"When I first got in the league, I didn't feel like I was taking a lot of threes," he said in early 2025. "It was the shot I was being told to take ... but off-the-dribble wasn't as much a thing, the deep ones wasn't a thing yet ... I think the better player I became and the more I worked at it, the more I started to shoot them."

Perhaps the biggest reason for the bump in volume is the shift in league personnel. More and more big men are shooting threes, which means that teams like the Celtics and others can play lineups where all five players are capable three-point shooters.

Golden State Warriors' Stephen Curry shoots a three-pointer during a game against the Minnesota Timberwolves on April 5, 2016. Curry was in the midst of a record-breaking regular season in which he set a still-untouchable record of 402 made threes.

"I think one of the things I think that's significant is the teams that have the highest numbers really shoot it at five positions. So you have centers that shoot in addition to everybody else, and I think that puts additional pressure on the defense," said Atlanta Hawks head coach Quin Snyder. "And I guess, like anything, you know, as it becomes more normal and more natural, certainly everybody knows that three is more than two, so you'd think that we'd get here sooner, but it's just the evolution of the game .... [but] if you lose that that battle, so to speak, even in terms of attempts it does get harder to win."

Another element is the type of threes teams are comfortable with their players taking. For a long time, the goal was to get wide-open, catch-and-shoot threes, preferably in the corners. But as the three became more and more mainstream, shooting them in transition or off the dribble became more common, something Boston in particular has leveraged.

"I don't think the volume of threes is necessarily the outlier, because everybody's taking a lot of threes," said Chicago Bulls head coach Billy Donovan, whose team was third in the NBA in threes taken in 2024–25. "I think the one thing that gets lost in all that is the volume of threes [Boston takes] off the dribble. That's the outlier. There's no team in the league that takes that many off the dribble. And I say that with all respect ... they have guys, you know, with Jayson Tatum and Jaylen Brown, that can shoot over you, you know, and they're elite at it ... so when you're playing them, it's not only like moving the ball and then getting catch-and-shoot threes. The reason the volume is so high is because they can take so many off the dribble, and their percentages really don't drop."

What was once a "revolution" is now normalized.

The greatest three-point shooter in NBA history is Curry. He breaks his own career mark for made threes every single time he scores one and owns the single-season record for makes — 402 — set in 2015–16, when he smashed his own record of 286 set the previous year by 116. At the time Curry was breaking new ground, becoming the first player in league history to attempt 10 or more threes a game.

But as a rookie in 2009–10 Curry attempted just 4.8 threes per game. Through his first six seasons he averaged just 6.5 attempts from deep, while converting an impressive 44 percent of them. Even in his first MVP season in 2014–15 Curry averaged "just" 8.1 three-point attempts per game. Meanwhile Victor Wembanyama, the San Antonio Spurs' 7-foot-3 center, was shooting 35.2 percent from deep and averaging 8.8 attempts in the 2024–25 season, his second in the league.

For Curry it's now a different world, even if he helped create it. In 2024–25 the Warriors star led the NBA in three-point attempts per game (11.2) for the ninth time in his career and finished third in made threes, but even he can't quite relate to a league rapidly being populated by shooters of all shapes and sizes who are getting shots up in a hurry and in large volume, with varying degrees of success.

Curry earned his three-point shooting stripes over time, learning his craft through experience, analysis and adaptation.

"It gave me confidence," Curry said in January 2025. "And everything is earned in the sense, like, even from Davidson [where he played three years of college basketball] when I was my freshman year to my junior year, there's a kind of a natural evolution to my game, and that's the beauty of how I experienced it. There wasn't anything forced. And I worked on it. I kind of started to see the pictures a little bit. I understand how it's being guarded, and how I can kind of influence the game, or impact the game, a little bit more. So the more you get into it, the more [you] start to kind of assess what works for you. If I came in my rookie year and just started flinging ... I don't think I would have adapted to ... or appreciated, you know, how hard it is to do what we have to do on a nightly basis, because it just wasn't my game at the time. So it was a natural progression of trying to reinvent your game."

The Celtics have reinvented themselves on a team-wide level. In their last year before Mazzulla took over as head coach at the start of the 2022–23 season, Boston had only three regulars taking 5 threes or more per game. In 2024–25 they had seven players in their rotation shooting at least 5 threes per game and an eighth, veteran guard Jrue Holiday, averaging 4.9. In many ways Boston represents where roster construction and tactics could be headed in that the Celtics feature centers who can shoot the long ball and a slew of wing players who have the ability and freedom to shoot threes off the dribble, which is how the team can routinely exceed the league average for attempts by 10 threes a game or more.

"I love three pointers. I like math," Mazzulla said on the eve of his first season as a head coach in 2022–23. "I like open threes, I like space and I think it's a huge strength of our team. So, the thing we have to learn on the offensive end is exactly what you said. Just making sure we're getting the best actual shot every time down, and regardless of if it goes in or not, it's a good shot."

Taking unprecedented volumes of threes is not the only way to play winning basketball in the NBA, but it's become a recipe that more teams are replicating and living with the results. ■

WINNERS

Jaylen Brown

Amica
CELTICS
7

Jaylen BROWN

POSITION SF, SG // **SHOOTS** RIGHT // **HEIGHT** 6'6" // **WEIGHT** 223 LBS // **DRAFTED** 2016, 3RD OVERALL

There is a difference between recognition and validation.

Jaylen Brown has earned his share of recognition throughout his career. It started when the Boston Celtics made him the No. 3 pick in the 2016 NBA Draft after one season at the University of California. He was an All-Rookie selection while coming off the bench on a deep Celtics team that won 53 games and advanced to the Eastern Conference Finals. In his second season, he was a starter on a 55-win team that made it to the Eastern Conference Finals again, losing for the second-straight season to LeBron James and the Cleveland Cavaliers.

By his fourth season, Brown was a 20-point-per-game scorer who made his third appearance in the Eastern Conference Finals, and by year five Brown was averaging 24.7 points per game as an NBA All Star.

At 6-foot-6 with an athletic energy reminiscent of a coiled spring and a ferocious competitive intensity at both ends of the floor, Brown quickly gained recognition as one of the best young players in the NBA.

But it took falling short on the NBA's brightest stage to set him on a trajectory that allowed him to reach greater heights.

After being in the playoffs for all five years of his career and being in the conference finals three times and falling short, it seemed fair to expect that the 2021–22 Finals was going to be the moment Brown and his Celtics co-star Jayson Tatum would finally get over the hump. Instead, the Celtics lost a crucial Game 4 at home while leading the series 2-1 and went on to be eliminated in six games by the veteran Golden State Warriors. Brown had some moments — he led Boston with 34 points in the Game 6 elimination game — but he made 10 turnovers in the last two games of the series as the Warriors forced him to his weaker left hand. He shot just 43.1 percent for the series.

But Brown used the disappointment to fuel him. He earned All-NBA honors for the first time in 2022–23, and the following season he was named an All Star for the third time.

In the 2023–24 Eastern Conference Finals, Brown took his game up one more level. In eliminating the Indiana Pacers in four games, Brown averaged 29.8 points, 5 rebounds and 3 assists on 51.7 percent shooting (and 37 percent from three) as he earned MVP honors for the series.

"Yeah, you learn and grow from your experiences, from being a 25-year-old to being a 27-year-old is a big difference," Brown said on the eve of his second Finals appearance, this time against Luka Doncic and

CAREER HIGHLIGHTS

- > 2023–24 NBA Champion
- > 2023–24 Finals MVP
- > 2023–24 Eastern Conference Finals MVP
- > 4-time All Star
- > 2022–23 All-NBA Second Team

the Dallas Mavericks. "Yeah, I'm 27 [smiling]. You learn from those experiences."

The Eastern Conference Finals MVP award was only another stepping stone. Brown was at his best in the first three games of the Finals, averaging 24.3 points, 6 rebounds, 5.7 assists, 2 steals and 1.3 blocks. He set the tone offensively and defensively against the Mavericks as the Celtics jumped to an insurmountable 3-0 lead on their way to winning the series in five games.

This time it was the Finals MVP award that Brown was accepting after the final horn. In his eighth season and his team's eighth playoff campaign, after advancing to the Eastern Conference Finals six times and the Finals twice, after 124 career playoff games, Brown earned one the highest honors in sports and a championship to go with it.

Brown has shared so many of those triumphs and pitfalls with Tatum. Combined they create the best wing tandem in the NBA and are marching side-by-side into Celtics lore. The first thing Brown did when winning the Finals MVP was to remind Tatum and everyone else, "We did this together."

When it came time for Tatum to celebrate his partner, he was not at a loss for words.

"The main goal for us was to win a championship," said Tatum. "We weren't — we didn't care who got Finals MVP. I know that I need him through this journey, and he needs

Jaylen Brown drives to the basket and scores in Game 6 of the second round of the playoffs on May 16, 2025.

me. So, you know, it was great to see him have that moment and share that moment with him. I'm extremely happy for him. Well deserved. That was big-time. He earned that."

Brown earned the validation that only comes from sacrifice, disappointment, perseverance and eventual triumph — something that counts more than any kind of individual recognition.

He showed his mettle again even as the Celtics fell short of defending their 2024 championship the following season. Facing elimination on home court in Game 5 of their second round series against the New York Knicks, and with Tatum out with an injury, Brown scored 26 points and a career-high — regular season and playoffs included — 12 assists against just 2 turnovers in a crucial win that extended the series.

It was another sign of growth that comes through challenge, a theme he'd touched on after earning the Finals MVP trophy.

"I think we learned. I think we learned from all of our mistakes," Brown said then. "All of our adversity has made us stronger, made us tougher. All season you could see it. We started from the jump. We made all the sacrifices. We played both ends of the ball at a high level. We didn't skip any steps. And this was the result.

"But all of those experiences, led to here. All of the moments where we came up short, we felt like we let the city down, let ourselves down, all of that compiled is how we get to this moment. And it makes it feel even that much better that we had to go through all the journey, the heartbreak, the embarrassment, the loss, to get to the mountaintop." ■

NEW YORK KNICKS

11 Jalen BRUNSON

POSITION PG, SG // **SHOOTS** LEFT // **HEIGHT** 6'2" // **WEIGHT** 190 LBS // **DRAFTED** 2018, 33RD OVERALL

Jalen Brunson was born for this.

Literally. The New York Knicks superstar point guard's father is Rick Brunson, who used to bring young Jalen to Knicks practices when the team's head coach, Tom Thibodeau, was as an assistant coach in the early 2000s.

Thibodeau (who was let go from the Knicks at the end of the 2024–25 season) later hired the elder Brunson as an assistant coach when Thibodeau got the top job in Chicago for the Bulls and again in Minnesota when Thibodeau was the head coach for the Timberwolves.

And the Knicks' president of basketball operations who hired Thibodeau in advance of the 2020–21 season and later signed Jalen Brunson to a four-year, $104 million contract to bring him from Dallas as a free agent in the summer of 2022? That would be Leon Rose, Rick Brunson's former agent and Jalen's godfather.

Meanwhile Sam Rose — Leon's son — is Jalen's agent.

No wonder when Jalen Brunson was asked about why he chose to join the Knicks in free agency it all came down to relationships and bonds formed over decades and cemented over time.

"That's been the major theme since I got here ... family," Brunson said in a first-person essay in *The Players' Tribune* after his first season in New York. "When it comes to what it means to me to be a part of this Knicks era, it all starts there."

The Knicks couldn't be happier, or luckier. But then again it was those ties that encouraged them to bet on Brunson in free agency. There weren't a lot of teams lining up to pay north of $100 million to a 6-foot-2 point guard who isn't blindingly quick or notably athletic — the main reason he was taken 33rd overall by Dallas in the 2018 draft even after winning his first national championship as a freshman at Villanova in 2016 and a second in 2018 while being named National Player of the Year.

Brunson came off the bench for most of his first three years in Dallas, but even as a starter in 2021–22 he was very much in the shadow of former Mavericks superstar Luka Doncic. The Mavericks reportedly could have signed Brunson to a four-year extension for $55 million before his last season in Dallas but weren't entirely convinced it was the right move. In the end Brunson signed with the Knicks to play with the team whose practice facility and locker room he had the run of as a preschooler and for people he'd known all his life.

It didn't take long for the lefty point guard to justify the Knicks' faith in him.

In his first season as the full-time starting point guard, Brunson was a revelation, posting then-career highs in points per game (24), assists (6.2), three-point percentage (41.6) and free throw attempts (5.8 per game) as the Knicks won 47 games — 10 more than the season before Brunson arrived. New York advanced to the second round of the playoffs for the first time in 10 years and just the second time since 2000, when Rick Brunson was playing for New York and Thibodeau was an assistant coach.

"He's exceeded my expectations," Knicks legend and longtime broadcaster Walt "Clyde" Frazier told NBA.com. "... He's not fast but he's quick. He uses his body very well, able to squeeze between the defenders for the angles to get his shot off. What he lacks for speed he gets his body in there. Can't foul him because he makes his free throws. Deadly from 5 to 8 feet. [He's among the league leaders] in drawing charges. Sacrifices his body."

His former head coach knew what he was getting when the Knicks signed him, but that doesn't mean he took Brunson for granted. "He's a team-first guy. He's always about all the right things," Thibodeau said. "The way he practices, the way he is in meetings, who he is as a person, I think that stuff's invaluable to a team. I've always been a big believer in the best leadership you can have are the things that you do each and every day ... you can tell what's important to him. Just watch him."

In 2023–24 Brunson had one of the best offensive seasons a point guard has ever had, logging 28.7 points and 6.7 assists while shooting 40.1 percent from three and making 211 triples — joining him with two-time MVP Steph Curry and NBA 75th anniversary team honoree Damian Lillard as the only point guards to ever hit those marks.

Jalen Brunson attempts to shoot over two Los Angeles Lakers defenders in a March 6, 2025, game.

CAREER HIGHLIGHTS

- 2024–25 Clutch Player of the Year
- 2-time All Star
- 2-time All-NBA Second Team

The Knicks won 50 games for the first time in 11 years, while Brunson was named an All Star for the first time in his career, finished fifth in MVP voting and earned All-NBA Second Team honors.

The Knicks were ravaged with injuries during the 2024 postseason, but that didn't prevent Brunson from helping them to the seventh game of the second round of the playoffs before falling to the Indiana Pacers. Over a five-game stretch from Game 6 of the first round against the Philadelphia 76ers through Game 4 of the second round against Indiana, Brunson scored 210 points — an average of 42 a game — which was the most by a player over five consecutive playoff games since Michael Jordan scored 215 in a five-game stretch in the 1993 postseason.

The next season Brunson picked up where he left off, leading the Knicks to a 51-win season and third seed in the Eastern Conference as he averaged 26 points and a career-best 7.3 assists while earning All-Star recognition and All-NBA Second Team honors. He also won the league's Clutch Player of the Year award as he led the NBA in averaging 5.6 points a game in the final five minutes and overtime periods of games that are within five points or less.

Brunson lived up to the award in the postseason. His clutch plays helped get the Knicks to their first conference finals in 25 years. In the first round, Brunson hit the series-winning three with 2.8 seconds left to cap off a 40-point game against the Detroit Pistons. In round two against the Boston Celtics, he scored 11 of his 29 points in the last quarter of Game 1 as he lifted the Knicks to a 20-point comeback win. The Knicks won the second round series in six games before they fell in six games to the Indiana Pacers in the conference finals.

The 2024–25 season was the Knicks' most successful season in a quarter century, and Brunson was in the middle of it, doing what he was born to do. ■

DENVER NUGGETS

32

Aaron GORDON

POSITION PF, SF // **SHOOTS** RIGHT // **HEIGHT** 6'8" // **WEIGHT** 235 LBS // **DRAFTED** 2014, 4TH OVERALL

Sometimes it's not the player, it's the situation.

Aaron Gordon's credentials entering the NBA could not be questioned. The burly high-flyer from Fresno, California, shone at every level anywhere he stepped on the floor. He led his high school to its first-ever state championship. He was twice the Player of the Year in California, where there is never a shortage of basketball talent. Playing for Team USA, he won tournament MVP honors at the U19 FIBA World Cup in 2013, notching a win over a potent Serbian team led by a largely unknown center, Nikola Jokic.

The successes continued, which was hardly surprising given there simply aren't many 6-foot-8, 235-pound forwards with good basketball IQ and the ability to put their head at rim level when they dunk, as Gordon was gaining a reputation for doing through his one college season at the University of Arizona, where he earned All-Conference honors as a freshman and led his team to the Elite Eight of the NCAA March Madness tournament in 2014.

And through his first five seasons with the Orlando Magic, who took him with the fourth pick in the 2014 draft, Gordon was assembling a nice NBA career. He had averages of 12.5 points, 6.2 rebounds and 2.2 assists while playing about 28 minutes a game. He was developing a reputation as a good defender. It was all perfectly respectable numbers a lot of NBA players would love to have beside their name.

Aaron Gordon dunks in a game on March 19, 2025, versus the Los Angeles Lakers.

But for Gordon, something was missing. The Magic didn't qualify for the playoffs for his first four seasons, and when they made it in his fifth season in 2018–19, Gordon played some of his best basketball against the eventual champion Toronto Raptors, but Orlando lost in five games in the first round. The following year the Magic squeaked into the playoffs again, despite winning just 33 games, and were once again eliminated in the first round. He played for five coaches and two general managers in six seasons in Central Florida. The Magic slid back into the draft lottery again in year seven, choosing to rebuild rather than chasing mediocrity.

Meanwhile Gordon was looking for change also, letting Orlando know he'd be open to being traded. He got his wish at the trade deadline in the 2020–21 season, and the Magic found a willing taker in the Denver Nuggets.

And Gordon? He found a home. He proved a perfect fit with the Nuggets, playing a central role in Denver's run to the 2022–23 NBA championship. He was the electrifying finisher for his old FIBA rival Jokic's seeing-eye passes, a "grab-and-go" rebounder and ball handler who helped spark the Nuggets in transition, and the perfect rugged, multipositional defender any team with championship aspirations requires.

"In many ways, Aaron is the heart and soul of the team," then-Nuggets general manager Calvin Booth told *The Athletic* after Gordon signed a four-year, $133 million contract extension in the summer of 2024. "He does a lot of things on the floor that makes us go. The guys rally around him in the locker room, and now with this agreement, we can move forward as a unit."

The Nuggets would be eliminated by Oklahoma City in the second round of the 2024–25 playoffs, but not before pushing the top-seeded Thunder to seven games. Gordon further cemented his place in Nuggets lore with plays like his game-winning putback dunk in Game 4 of Denver's first-round series against the Los Angeles Clippers, his game-winning three in Game 1 against OKC and his three to force overtime in Game 3, leading to another Nuggets victory. He then showed the full range of his grit when he suited up for Game 7 despite suffering a Grade 2 hamstring strain in Game 6.

Over the years Gordon has built connections with Jokic — the greatest passing big man to ever play basketball — and his Nuggets teammates that run deeper than his Denver averages of 15 points, 6 rebounds and 3 assists would suggest. He was miscast in Orlando, where they wanted him to be a primary scorer and creator. Turns out his best role in the NBA is as a star role player, the type of competitor who lifts a group by making his success about team success.

"That's who I do it for," Gordon said during the 2023 NBA Finals. "Every day when I feel like I'm tired, and I feel like I don't want to work out and I don't want to get that extra rep in, I just think of Nikola and I think of Jamal [Murray] and I think of Michael [Porter Jr.] and [former Nugget Kentavious Caldwell-Pope] and the guys in this locker room, and I make sure I do it for them. That gives me the energy I need to finish strong."

Gordon was bound for NBA success — his track record told that story. He just needed the right environment, and he found it in the Mile High City. ■

CAREER HIGHLIGHTS

> 2022–23 NBA Champion

3 Josh HART

POSITION SF, SG // **SHOOTS** RIGHT // **HEIGHT** 6'4" // **WEIGHT** 215 LBS // **DRAFTED** 2017, 30TH OVERALL

The ultimate currency in the NBA is minutes played.

If the level you play helps your team's cause, your minutes increase. It's the simplest and truest statistic in the sport.

And by that measure, there are few players in the NBA more valuable to their team than Josh Hart — the athletic, energetic and tireless do-everything wing for the New York Knicks.

After the Knicks acquired the former Villanova University star at the trade deadline during the 2022–23 season, Hart became one of the team's workhorses, averaging 30 minutes a game off the bench for a Knicks team that lost in the second round of the 2023 playoffs to the Miami Heat.

But the demands on Hart — and what he was able to give — went to another level the following season as injuries hit the Knicks' rotation. On March 18, 2024, Hart became just the third player in franchise history to play all 48 minutes in a game. In the win over the Golden State Warriors, Hart recorded his fifth career triple-double, with 10 points, 11 rebounds and 11 assists.

But Hart's Iron Man feats were just beginning. Over the first nine games of the Knicks' injury-plagued run to the second round of the 2024 postseason, Hart *averaged* 46.4 minutes per game. In four of those games he didn't leave the floor for even a minute.

"I would say it's because he saves it from not practicing. He competes during the games," longtime teammate Jalen Brunson joked when asked where Hart's energy is derived. "So yeah, I don't know, man. The dude's crazy. It's how he's wired."

Brunson would know, given he played two seasons with Hart at Villanova, winning a national championship with him (and fellow Knick Mikal Bridges) in 2015–16, before Hart graduated as an All-American in 2016–17 and was taken 30th overall in the 2017 draft by the Utah Jazz and traded to the Los Angeles Lakers.

Over the next eight seasons Hart made himself the kind of player coaches loath to take off the floor.

There is no better indicator of Hart's approach than his status as one of the best rebounding guards in the NBA. Hart, who averaged a career-best 9.6 rebounds during the 2024–25 season, is one of only two guards in the league to have a total rebound percentage of better than 13 percent since 2019–20 — the other being Lakers star Luka Doncic.

At 6-foot-4, his ability to grab rebounds is a tribute to not only his athleticism but also an uncommon level of tenacity and willfulness.

"First of all, his heart is as big as Texas," said Portland Trail Blazers head coach Chauncy Billups, who coached Hart for parts of two seasons before he was traded to the Knicks. "You've got to have the will and the grit to go in there and do that. Most of the time you're undersized and you've got to actually steal those rebounds from dudes that are bigger than you. So it's a gift, it's nothing I can teach. He brought that. None of us get credit for that, it's just who he is. He has a knack for the basketball.

Hart credits his ability to track the basketball to his background in baseball, but the rest he attributes to his nature. He's relentless, constantly looking for a way to get from point A to point B a little quicker. The ball being there when he arrives is the prize.

"I think part of it is mentality, part is being able to track it," Hart said once in an interview with NBA.com while he was in Portland. "That's the biggest thing. I played baseball when I was a kid, so I was playing outfield and obviously with that, you're tracking, seeing where the ball is going and all those kinds of things. That's something I'm always doing, I'm always thinking that way, even when I'm driving in traffic. I'm like, 'If I go in this lane ...' My wife doesn't like it because I probably be speeding. I'm like, 'If I can go this way, I can do this ...' You know what I mean? I'm always trying to measure where I can go, where the ball is going to go, where I can fit and all those kinds of things. Stuff like that, that's interesting to me."

Hart led all NBA guards in rebounding in 2024–25 with a career-best 9.6 per game and led the league in minutes per game with 37.6. His 1.5 steals per game was a career-best and ranked him eighth-best league-wide among players with at least 65 games played.

Hart does things that are foundational to winning, and coaches can't help but love players who contribute to winning — and those same coaches love to play those players.

"I think [Hart] is a big-time multiple-effort guy," then-Knicks head coach Tom Thibodeau said shortly after Hart arrived in New York. "He's gonna keep going. He'll give you a second and third effort to go get it."

Josh Hart shoots over Indiana Pacers guard Andrew Nembhard in a game on February 11, 2025.

CAREER HIGHLIGHTS

- 2024–25 Minutes Per Game Leader (37.6)

BOSTON CELTICS

42 Al HORFORD

POSITION C // **SHOOTS** RIGHT // **HEIGHT** 6'9" // **WEIGHT** 240 LBS // **DRAFTED** 2007, 3RD OVERALL

In professional sports, you get what you deserve.

In theory.

But the reality is that at the highest levels of competition, just being deserving isn't enough. There is too much talent. Too many equally deserving players. Not everyone gets to call themselves a champion.

Which is why Al Horford finally earning the honor following the 2023–24 season with the Boston Celtics was so special. Horford, at the time a 17-year-veteran, had to play 186 playoff games before he could finally raise the Larry O'Brien Trophy. Only Karl Malone, the former Utah Jazz great and Hall of Famer played more (193) without winning a title, and he retired in 2004 having played in three NBA Finals but never winning a ring.

Malone was deserving. As was his longtime teammate and Hall of Famer John Stockton (182), Indiana Pacers great Reggie Miller (144) and countless other NBA stars who didn't get to win the last game of the postseason over their long and illustrious careers.

No one questioned whether Horford was capable of being central to a championship team or not. He came into the NBA as the No. 3–overall pick in 2007, in part because of his role leading the University of Florida to consecutive NCAA titles in 2006 and 2007. In the NBA Horford's teams in Atlanta and Boston — with brief stops in Philadelphia and Oklahoma City — made the postseason in 15 of his first 17 seasons.

Al Horford blocks a shot by Phoenix Suns star Devin Booker on April 4, 2025.

Finally getting over the hump in Boston made it all the sweeter. In Horford's five previous years in the green and white, the Celtics had fallen short in the Eastern Conference Finals three times, the Finals once and the second round once.

"The first thing you have to do when you come here is you have to embrace that pressure," Horford said after Boston finally broke through in a five-game series win over the Dallas Mavericks. "And I was okay with being in that position. I was okay if we were getting criticized and we weren't getting it done because I understood what it means playing here. Finally overcoming that and winning and putting ourselves with the greats, this is special."

The crowd at Boston's TD Garden understood the significance when Celtics head coach Joe Mazzulla — three years Horford's junior — subbed out Horford with 2:02 remaining in the fourth quarter of the deciding game with the championship well in hand. The crowd's ovation spoke volumes.

"Nobody deserved it more than Al," said Finals MVP Jaylen Brown. "He's been a great leader not just on the court but off the court as well ... It's been an honor to be by his side. And Al Horford is a real-life legend and hero. It's been great to be his teammate."

And Horford was more than a ceremonial figure. He was thrust into a starting role when Kristaps Porzingis got injured, and he delivered some signature performances: notching 22 points, 15 rebounds and 5 assists in a close-out win over Cleveland in the second round and 23 points, 5 rebounds and 3 blocks in a Game 3 win over Indiana in the Eastern Conference Finals to put Boston in position to sweep. In Game 5 against Dallas, Horford added in 9 points, 9 rebounds, 2 assists and 2 steals — one of which brought the Boston crowd to their feet when he dove on the floor to recover a loose ball before flipping it to Brown for the score.

"We leaned on him so much," Brown said. "Probably too much for his age and where he's at. He just delivered. So consistent, so disciplined with his body. Never complains, you know what I mean. The only thing he does is add to winning."

It made for a fitting exclamation point on a superb career. Horford, who is also the first Dominican-born player to win an NBA title, is a five-time All Star who has been recognized as an All-NBA defender and was named to the All-NBA Third Team in 2011.

All along he's expanded and evolved his game. Horford attempted just 29 threes through his first seven seasons, but as the need to space the floor for the modern NBA offense increased, Horford adapted. In seasons nine through 16, Horford took 2,210 of his field goal attempts from behind the arc and converted them at a rate of 38.1 percent, establishing himself as one of the best shooting big men of his generation.

Not that statistics — or his age — have ever defined Horford. He returned for his 18th season in 2024–25 and helped lead Boston to the playoffs again, his 16th time in the postseason. After a 61-win regular season, Boston was upset by the New York Knicks in a six-game second-round series. But Horford did his part: at age 38 he was third on the team in minutes played during the playoffs, shot 40 percent from the three-point line and led Boston in blocked shots.

When the time finally comes for him to retire, his career averages won't figure too prominently in his career retrospective, though averaging 12.9 points, 7.9 rebounds, 3.2 assists and 1.1 blocks through his first 18 seasons is nothing to be taken lightly. Instead Horford will be remembered for his all-around excellence, as a beloved and respected teammate and, finally, as a deserving champion. ■

CAREER HIGHLIGHTS

- 2023–24 NBA Champion
- 5-time All Star
- 2010–11 All-NBA Third Team
- 2017–18 All-Defensive Second Team
- 2007–08 All-Rookie First Team

DENVER NUGGETS

27 Jamal MURRAY

POSITION PG, SG // **SHOOTS** RIGHT // **HEIGHT** 6'4" // **WEIGHT** 215 LBS // **DRAFTED** 2016, 7TH OVERALL

Legends Are Made in the Postseason: The Jamal Murray Story.

The Denver Nuggets guard has never made an All-Star team. He's never been mentioned as a possible All-NBA selection or even been Player of the Month.

Which isn't to say he's not an excellent NBA player. The seventh pick in the 2016 draft, Murray averaged 20.9 points, 5.9 assists and 1.2 steals while shooting 40.5 percent on 6 three-point attempts a game since his breakout 2020–21 season through the 2024–25 season, a period that includes his lost 2021–22 season, during which he was out with an ACL injury.

The only other guard to average at least 20.9 points and 5.9 assists a game over that stretch while converting more than 40 percent of their threes is Steph Curry. But Murray's postseason accomplishments more than make up for the fact that his regular-season performances haven't come with individual recognition.

Through his first three playoff runs with the Nuggets, Murray averaged 25 points, 5 rebounds and 6.3 assists. In so doing he joined Michael Jordan, LeBron James, Jerry West, Curry, Giannis Antetokounmpo and Nikola Jokic as the only players to hit those thresholds with at least 50 games of postseason action.

As the Nuggets won their first NBA championship in franchise history in 2023, Murray joined Jordan, Magic Johnson and James as the only players in league history to average at least 20 points and 10 assists in the Finals, which Murray managed in Denver's five-game win over the Miami Heat.

Heading into those Finals his teammate Jokic said it was Murray who was the most responsible for lifting their team to new heights.

"He averaged 30 points, a great percentage [in the Western Conference Finals]. I think that's really hard to do, especially that high number of points," said Jokic, who later added a Finals MVP award to go with the two MVP awards he had earned to that point. "But not just points. I think his energy, I would say even from the first round, his energy, he's been our best player since round one … even if he doesn't make shots … his energy is always good. I think that's the best feeling for the guys around him. You know, yes, we know he can make shots, he can go for 50. But even when things doesn't go his way, he doesn't fall down. He is still playing. He's still fighting …"

From Murray's view, his playoff performances and championship ring make the All-Star snubs easier to swallow.

"Obviously, I would love to be an All Star," he said in an interview with *The Athletic* after he was passed over for the Western Conference All-Star team in 2024–25. "I'd love to get that kind of recognition. But I think when you win in the playoffs ... and show yourself on the biggest stages and you prove yourself against those so-called All Stars, [then it's] whatever ..."

Proving himself has been Murray's mantra since he started turning heads as a promising prospect out of Kitchener, a mid-sized city about an hour west of Toronto — hardly known as a basketball hotbed.

He made his Toronto debut as a teenager at the Jane and Finch Classic, a highly competitive community event played for local bragging rights, where the action on the floor is often matched by the energy of the crowd.

"I mean, most kids, when you bring them to that environment, they crumble, you know?" said Mike George a prominent Amateur Athletic Union coach at the time and eventually Murray's agent. "They're not used to, like, grown men in the stands yelling, 'Yo, you suck' and yelling different things. It's intimidating to be around them dudes, and he was like, 'Nope, you're going to know my name by the time I leave this building' and they sure did."

After playing one season at the University of Kentucky, Murray was drafted by Denver with the seventh pick in the 2016 draft, but he only put himself on the NBA map during the Nuggets' playoff run at the end of the 2019–20 season, which was held in the league's "bubble" in Orlando during the pandemic.

In leading the Nuggets to the Western Conference Finals against the eventual champion LA Lakers, he averaged 26.5 points and 6.6 assists while shooting 45.3 percent from three. His run included a three-game stretch in the first round when Murray scored 50, 42 and 50 points in consecutive games as the Nuggets came back from being down 3-1 to win their first-round series over the Utah Jazz. In the second round, he averaged 29 points and 5.7 assists in Games 5, 6 and 7 as Denver once again clawed back a 3-1 deficit to topple the LA Clippers.

The Nuggets lost in seven games in the second-round of the 2024–25 playoffs to the Oklahoma City Thunder, but not before Murray added to his résumé of signature postseason moments, such as his 43-point explosion in a crucial Game 5 win over the Clippers in the first round, or his battle through the flu and a ruthless OKC defense to scratch out 25 points, 8 rebounds and 7 assists and stave off elimination at home in Game 6 of the second round.

"I think what can maybe allow Jamal to rest at nighttime is he's done things in the playoffs that guys who have been All Stars will never do," said then-Nuggets head coach Michael Malone in April 2024.

"That's not just winning a championship, but 50-point games, putting the team on his back and truly showing up and showing out on the world's biggest stage ... whether he's an All Star or not, we know that he's a great player and a huge part of any and all success that we have." ■

Jamal Murray rises to shoot over Oklahoma City Thunder center Jaylin Williams in Game 3 of the second round of the playoffs on May 9, 2025.

CAREER HIGHLIGHTS

- 2022–23 NBA Champion
- 2016–17 All-Rookie Second Team

Pascal SIAKAM

POSITION PF // **SHOOTS** RIGHT // **HEIGHT** 6'8" // **WEIGHT** 230 LBS // **DRAFTED** 2017, 27TH OVERALL

Pascal Siakam lays up the ball in Game 6 of the Eastern Conference Finals against the New York Knicks on May 31, 2025.

Quality travels.

Pascal Siakam's basketball journey has taken him across oceans, cultures and languages with the speed of a rocket ship. From his native Cameroon to the heart of Texas to the shadow of the Mexican border to Canada and, finally, to Indianapolis, Indiana, the heart of the U.S. Midwest.

And at every step it has been Siakam's unique combination of abilities and determination that has enabled him to stand out, forge ahead and finally arrive at what feels like his forever basketball home.

"For me, it just felt like, man, I'm excited about the future here," Siakam said when he signed as a free agent with the Pacers in the summer of 2024. He had been traded to Indiana in the middle of the 2023–24 season from the Toronto Raptors. "And when I felt like that excitement was the same thing on the organization's part, it just felt like an easy decision."

Prior to the trade to Indiana, Siakam had established himself with the Raptors through seven full seasons and earned recognition with the NBA's Most Improved Player award in 2019, All-NBA seasons in 2019–20 and 2021–22 and All-Star appearances in 2020 and 2024. Not to mention he also played a crucial role in Toronto's 2019 championship run. Since joining the Pacers though, Siakam's comfort level has been apparent. It was a franchise-defining move for Indiana, and his transition was instant and seamless.

Over 41 regular-season games after the trade, Siakam averaged 21.3 points, 7.8 rebounds and 3.7 assists while shooting 54.6 percent from the field and 38.6 percent from three-point range. He showed his quality again in the playoffs when he lent leadership and stability to a young Pacers team still getting their feel for postseason basketball.

In the opening game of the Pacers' 2024 first-round playoff series against the Milwaukee Bucks, Siakam demonstrated his postseason pedigree with a pair of masterpieces, both on the road against the favored Bucks: 36 points and 13 rebounds on 15-of-25 shooting in a Game 1 loss and 37 points, 11 rebounds and 6 assists on 16-of-23 shooting in a Game 2 win that helped set the stage for Indiana's first-round upset. The two-game explosion, during which Siakam exceeded his previous playoff career high of 34 points, which he set with the Raptors in 2019, made the Pacers' forward the first player since Wilt Chamberlain to open the postseason with consecutive games of at least 35 points and 10 rebounds.

By the time the postseason was over the Pacers had exceeded everyone's expectations (other than perhaps their own) by reaching the Eastern Conference Finals for the first time in a decade, and it was clear Siakam was going to be part of Indiana's future.

"This is a historic day," Pacers head coach Rick Carlisle said when Siakam signed a four-year deal for $189 million in summer 2024. "This is easily the biggest free agent signing in the history of this franchise."

For Siakam it was another stage in one of the most remarkable basketball journeys in the annals of the NBA.

Siakam grew up wanting to be a soccer star in Cameroon, playing basketball only recreationally and occasionally. But as an exceptionally tall and athletic 18-year-old, he was identified as a promising player and invited to a Basketball Without Borders camp in South Africa, which he only attended so he could visit his sister who lived there.

From there he attended a prep school in Texas and earned a scholarship at New Mexico State.

Despite being 6-foot-8 and close to 230 pounds with exceptional quickness and mobility, he was still raw and so he redshirted in his first season. By his second college season — still technically a freshman — he was First-Team All-Conference, and by his sophomore season he led the Western Athletic Conference in scoring (20.1 per game), rebounding (11.3) and blocks (2) while earning Player of the Year honors. Siakam was taken 27th overall by the Raptors in the 2016 draft and was announced as a starter in the first NBA game he had ever played in. By his third season he was the second-leading scorer on an NBA championship team, and by his fourth season he was an All Star and an All-NBA Second Team member, averaging 22.9 points, 7.3 rebounds and 3.5 assists for a Raptors team that was on pace for 60 wins, were it not for a pandemic-shortened season.

In sum, in the space of eight years Siakam went from a recreational player with no formal basketball experience to a pro with All-NBA status.

His trajectory has continued in Indiana. In 2024–25, he followed up his impressive first half-season by being named an All Star for the third time and averaging 20.2 points, 6.9 rebounds and 3.4 assists while shooting a career-best 38.9 percent from three in just 32 minutes a game for a Pacers team that earned home court advantage in the first round of the playoffs. Siakam went on to lead Indiana to the NBA Finals for the first time since 1999–2000. They eventually lost to the Oklahoma City Thunder in seven games, but not before Siakam earned the Larry Bird Trophy as Eastern Conference Finals MVP after averaging 24.8 points per game with an effective field goal percentage of 57.1 as the Pacers upset the Knicks in six games.

For Siakam it was the seventh time he had helped take his team to the postseason in nine years, and the second straight with his new team, with the prospect of more to come.

CAREER HIGHLIGHTS

- > 2018–19 NBA Champion
- > 2024–25 Eastern Conference Finals MVP
- > 2018–19 Most Improved Player
- > 3-time All Star
- > 2019–20 All-NBA Second Team

ORLANDO MAGIC

4 Jalen SUGGS

POSITION SG, PG // **SHOOTS** RIGHT // **HEIGHT** 6'5" // **WEIGHT** 205 LBS // **DRAFTED** 2021, 5TH OVERALL

It's not often that players taken in the top five of the NBA draft become celebrated as role players.

The top of the lottery is where teams hope to find All Stars, All-NBA players, athletes that shift the trajectory of a franchise.

Jalen Suggs of the Orlando Magic has proven to be the exception: a top-five pick who fulfills a lot of the responsibilities of a player taken that high — driving winning the foremost among them — but does it by doing all the things a role player does, albeit one infused with star-level talent.

It speaks to his character, which is perhaps his most important quality, ahead of his rugged, springy athleticism and dogged competitiveness.

"Without hesitation, I'll do anything the boys ask me to do," he explained in an interview with *The Ringer* during his breakout third season in 2023–24. "I'll try my hardest to get it done. I knew it would lead to good things for us … taking on that challenge. And I know it's hard, but it's a privilege that they … believe in me."

The 6-foot-5 guard found himself in what could have been an awkward situation after the Magic selected him fifth overall in the 2021 draft after he led Gonzaga to the NCAA Final, famously hitting a game-winning shot from 40 feet to win the national semifinal in overtime.

Taken three spots behind Suggs with the eighth pick was Franz Wagner out of Michigan. And it didn't take long for Wagner to emerge as the rookie more capable of being a traditional offense-generating star (although Suggs' rookie season was interrupted so regularly with injuries it was hard to get a handle on exactly how his talents would transfer to the NBA level). Then, prior to Suggs' second season, the Magic won the draft lottery and selected Duke star Paolo Banchero with the first overall pick, nudging Suggs one more notch down the pecking order.

Some players with Suggs' pedigree might have bristled at the situation he found himself in — on a team where, by default, he wasn't the primary offensive option, the moon around which everyone else orbited.

Instead Suggs embraced another path, becoming a willing and determined supporter of his teammates and channeling his innate fire and physicality — in addition to being a high school basketball star in Minnesota he was the state's best football player — into being one of the best defensive players in the NBA.

After two rebuilding seasons during which Suggs struggled at times with consistency in large part due to injury (he missed 34 games in his first season and 29 in his second), he demonstrated his impact in his third season when he helped Orlando to 47 wins in 2023–24, their most successful season in 13 years — all of it based on a suffocating, aggressive and physical brand of team defense that was rated third in the NBA, with Suggs as the catalyst.

"He's the head of our defense when it comes to picking up the basketball, getting into the ball, turning teams over," said Orlando Magic head coach Jamahl Mosley. "His defensive intensity, that's probably a good word to use, as well as energy. He has an intensity about him when he's guarding the basketball. He has [this] ability to push the ball in transition after we get major stops, and then he's just aggressive and fearless in a lot of ways when it comes to attacking a basket. And that's a different energy, that he does provide, a different intensity to the game."

That 2023–24 season, he led the Magic and was among the NBA's leaders in total steals (10th), deflections (15th) and loose balls recovered on the defensive end (13th) and — almost certainly — he was among the league leaders in throwing his body around with sheer abandon in an effort to get the ball back for his team.

Jalen Suggs defensively pressures Jalen Brunson of the New York Knicks in a December 15, 2024, game.

CAREER HIGHLIGHTS

> 2023–24 All-Defensive Second Team

Suggs' efforts were recognized with an All-Defensive Second Team nod, and he found his footing offensively, too, as he averaged a then-career-best 12.6 points a game and — significantly, given that he has to play off of the ball so much with Wagner and Banchero as the hubs of the Magic's offense — 39.7 percent from three. Seemingly against the odds Orlando pushed the favored Cleveland Cavaliers to seven games in the first round of the 2024 playoffs.

It was no surprise that the Magic were considered dark-horse favorites to disrupt the Eastern Conference in 2024–25 as a young, improving team with the kind of tough, defensive identity traditionally required to thrive in the playoffs.

Suggs responded to the heightened expectations with career-best marks in points (16.2), assists (3.7), rebounds (4) and steals (1.5) while continuing to drive the Magic's defensive identity. With Suggs on the floor the Magic allowed only 104.8 points per 100 possessions, which would be the top-ranked defense in the league, according to the NBA's data. But when Suggs wasn't on the court, the Magic allowed 110.1 points per 100 possessions. That would rank as the league's sixth-best defense — still very good, of course, but not elite.

The only problem is that injuries were again an issue for the fourth-year guard. He was limited to just 35 games before his season ended in early March 2025 due to surgery to remove a cartilage fragment from his left knee.

But Suggs' role has been established — he's a superstar in it — and the Magic's future remains bright because of him. ■

5 Fred VANVLEET

POSITION PG, SG // **SHOOTS** RIGHT // **HEIGHT** 6'0" // **WEIGHT** 197 LBS // **DRAFTED** 2016, UNDRAFTED

Defining most NBA players' best attributes is usually pretty easy, especially for really good players. Filling up a box score isn't the only measure of player quality, but it's often a handy place to start. And typically the best players score a good amount of points, or grab rebounds in big numbers, or total up a lot of assists. The best of those are able to do it at higher volumes with greater efficiency on winning teams: see Nikola Jokic, Shai Gilgeous-Alexander, Giannis Antetokounmpo or others who are among the NBA's elite.

On the other hand, some players can impact a game and do it for winning teams — and are often a driving force on winning teams — but the specific reasons are a little harder to pin down.

Take Houston Rockets guard Fred VanVleet, for example. Since becoming a regular starter in his fourth season with the Toronto Raptors in 2019–20 through his second season in Houston in 2024–25, VanVleet has certainly been productive, averaging 18.1 points and ranking 11th in total assists (2,536) and second in total steals (616). In 2021–22, he managed to earn an All-Star nod when he averaged a career-high 20.3 points along with 6.7 assists and 1.7 steals while shooting 37.7 percent on nearly 10 three-point attempts per game on a Raptors team that exceeded expectations and won 48 games.

But what VanVleet does best are the things that are hard to count: lead, compete and stay calm under pressure.

"Fred is a dog, man," said Chris Paul, the Hall of Fame–bound point guard who VanVleet has modeled parts of his game after. "What I like about Fred is he doesn't back down. I play with a chip on my shoulder, he plays with a chip on his shoulder. I've always respected that about Fred. Not only is he nice [offensively], but he plays both ways. I'm one of the biggest Fred VanVleet fans there is."

But what VanVleet represents as much as anything is that there is a path to a long and successful NBA career that isn't paved by outrageous athletic gifts — standing just 6 feet tall, VanVleet's next dunk will be the first of his career — or by virtue of being tagged as a "prospect" from a young age.

Even as a star high school player in Rockford, Illinois, VanVleet was lightly recruited; his scholarship at Wichita State was one of the few he was offered. And even after having one of the best college careers possible at a mid-major school — over his four years VanVleet's teams went 123-24 and made it to the NCAA Tournament every year, advancing to the Final Four once, to the Sweet 16 twice and to the second round another time — he went undrafted.

After signing as a free agent with Toronto it didn't take him long to prove his value as he helped lead Toronto's G-League team to a championship in 2016–17. In 2017–18 VanVleet became an NBA regular and finished third in the Sixth Man of the Year voting as he helped the Raptors to a franchise record 59-win season. When the Raptors won the NBA title in 2019, VanVleet was a central figure in both the Eastern Conference Finals and the Finals. He came off the bench to shoot 52.6 percent from three in the final three games against the Milwaukee Bucks and the six-game series against the Golden State Warriors. He saved his best for last, scoring 12 of his 22 points in the fourth quarter of Toronto's championship-clinching victory, a series in which he successfully helped hold Warriors star Steph Curry to just 40.3 percent shooting over the final three games.

When the Raptors headed toward a rebuild, the Houston Rockets came hard at VanVleet in free agency in the summer of 2023, hoping he would bring his brand of toughness, IQ and maturity to their young locker room.

"I think I'm good for people who want to be great and who can be held accountable and who see the bigger picture," VanVleet said of his leadership style. "Guys that just care about winning, like, we're gonna never have an issue. The guys who have to learn how to do that, that's when it can be a little bumpy. [But] ... I just tell them the truth. First of all, 'This is what it takes. You might not like it right now, but you'll see it eventually. This is how you're going to get better. This is how you're going to get paid. This is how we're going to win. And I'm not lying to you.' I'm going to share what I've seen in my experience ... and hope that they can grasp it."

Fred VanVleet hustles for a loose ball in Game 7 of the first round of the playoffs on May 4, 2025.

CAREER HIGHLIGHTS

- 2018–19 NBA Champion
- 2022 All Star

The Rockets had won just 59 games — averaging out to less than 20 per season — in the three years before the team added VanVleet and a small core of other tough-minded veterans to help their team mature. In VanVleet's first season there (2023–24), the Rockets improved to 41 wins. In his second season they won 52 games and earned the second seed in the Western Conference before falling to the veteran Golden State Warriors in a seven-game series that Houston was trailing 3-1 before VanVleet heated up, averaging 24 points and 4.3 assists on 61.1 percent shooting from three over the last three games as the Rockets stormed back.

His performance showed that the gritty guard can ramp up his offense when needed, but for the most part VanVleet's role with Houston is to provide a calm, steady veteran presence, and he did it well. Even as he posted his lowest regular-season scoring average since 2018–19, he led the team in minutes and the Rockets were 3.3 points better per 100 possessions when he was on the floor versus when he was off.

"He's been everything [we were hoping for] and more, honestly," said Rockets head coach Ime Udoka. "... He checks all the boxes as far as toughness, leadership, edge, IQ, just in general ... he's happy with whatever comes his way as long as we win and so, that rubs off on our guys and that's the type of leader and point guard that we want." ■

Derrick WHITE

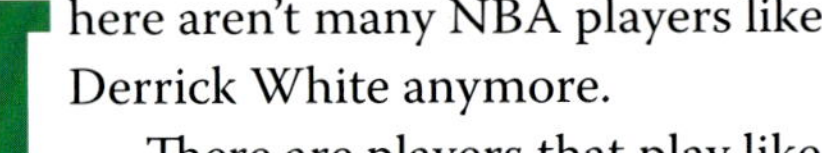

POSITION SG, PG // **SHOOTS** RIGHT // **HEIGHT** 6'4" // **WEIGHT** 190 LBS // **DRAFTED** 2017, 29TH OVERALL

There aren't many NBA players like Derrick White anymore.

There are players that play like White: smart, versatile, unselfish, capable of impacting games offensively and defensively, elite role players — in other words, some of the most valuable pieces a winning team can have.

But players who have walked a mile in the Boston Celtics guard's sneakers?

There aren't many of them. Most players who reach the NBA have been stars since sixth grade, with reputations to match; never more so in an era when youth basketball highlights are commoditized on social media even before those players reach high school.

That wasn't White's path. There was nothing about where his basketball journey began that would have predicted where he finally arrived — as a crucial starter on a Boston Celtics team that won the 2023–24 NBA championship having just missed winning it in 2022.

Since White was acquired from San Antonio at the trade deadline in 2022, Boston has barely missed a step, and White has carved out a niche as one of the NBA's best and most versatile role players.

For a player who didn't get a Division I scholarship offer coming out of high school and whose big break was catching the eye of the head coach of a Division II school best known for its culinary program, his success is a tribute to self-belief and his own determination.

"Just don't give up. Keep going. Keep working," White said when he first graced the Finals stage in 2022. "Enjoy what you do. I love basketball. So, I kept doing it. Good things started happening for me. So, do what you do."

What White does is a little bit of everything. During the Celtics' championship season, White's box score averages were relatively modest as he put up 15.2 points, 5.2 assists and 4.2 rebounds. But he did it efficiently — his 61.1 True Shooting percentage made him one of just 10 guards who were that efficient with their scoring while playing more than 2,200 minutes on the season, and he was the only one of that group to earn All-Defensive honors.

"Derrick is special," was Celtics veteran Al Horford's assessment. "Derrick is such a special player. He's a winner. He wants to be in these positions and these moments. It's just unbelievable how he continues to find ways to impact the game. Offense, defense, whatever it is, he's doing something to impact winning."

Derrick White blocks a shot by Cade Cunningham of the Detroit Pistons in a game on December 4, 2024, in Boston.

CAREER HIGHLIGHTS

- 2023–24 NBA Champion
- 2-time All-Defensive Second Team

He came perilously close to never having the chance. White was a late bloomer growing up in south Denver. He was a good player — he averaged 20 points a game at Legends High School and was an honorable mention for the All-State team — but as a skinny 6-footer, he was deemed too small and unathletic for college basketball. He got a Division II opportunity as a walk-on at the University of Colorado at Colorado Springs, but he had to pay his own tuition. Things began to change when White went through a late growth spurt. He was 6-foot-4 as a freshman and earned Freshman of the Year honors. By his junior season he was one of the best Division II players in the United States. He sat out a season and transferred to the University of Colorado to test himself against Division I competition and shone there, too, earning All-Conference honors. By that time the NBA had taken notice of the rangy, athletic kid with the all-round game, and the San Antonio Spurs drafted him 29th overall in 2017.

After four improving seasons in San Antonio came his next career twist: the Spurs were pivoting toward a rebuild, while the Celtics were looking for one more piece to help push them to the top of the NBA mountain. Celtics president and general manager Brad Stevens had good insight into White through then-Celtics head coach Ime Udoka, who was a Spurs assistant coach when White was in San Antonio.

To Stevens, White's ability to pass, shoot and defend made him the perfect complement to a team built around Jayson Tatum and Jaylen Brown.

"I think the analysis ... is we have some really good players, and we have a person that we think fits in perfectly with them as another really good player that can only make them better," Stevens said when the Celtics acquired White.

White's profile as a role-playing star has only continued to grow — so much so that shortly after the Celtics' championship parade was over, White's offseason was interrupted: he was an injury replacement for Kawhi Leonard on Team USA for the Paris Olympics.

After another solid season with the Celtics in 2024–25, White rose to the occasion in the playoffs, going off for 30 points in a series-opening win against the Orlando Magic and then saving the Celtics' season in the second round — albeit briefly — as he scored 34 points in a Game 5 win over the New York Knicks with Boston facing elimination. Without superstar Jayson Tatum, who suffered a season-ending Achilles tendon injury in Game 4, the short-handed Celtics were eliminated in six games, missing out on their chance to defend their title, but White proved again he can be counted on in the biggest moments.

From Division II walk-on to NBA champion to Olympic gold medalist, White is on a route not many basketball players have taken, but one where he has never missed a step. ■

NBA REGULAR-SEASON MVPs

2024–25: Shai Gilgeous-Alexander, Oklahoma City Thunder

2023–24: Nikola Jokic, Denver Nuggets

2022–23: Joel Embiid, Philadelphia 76ers

2021–22: Nikola Jokic, Denver Nuggets

2020–21: Nikola Jokic, Denver Nuggets

2019–20: Giannis Antetokounmpo, Milwaukee Bucks

2018–19: Giannis Antetokounmpo, Milwaukee Bucks

2017–18: James Harden, Houston Rockets

2016–17: Russell Westbrook, Oklahoma City Thunder

2015–16: Stephen Curry, Golden State Warriors

2014–15: Stephen Curry, Golden State Warriors

2013–14: Kevin Durant, Oklahoma City Thunder

2012–13: LeBron James, Miami Heat

2011–12: LeBron James, Miami Heat

2010–11: Derrick Rose, Chicago Bulls

2009–10: LeBron James, Cleveland Cavaliers

2008–09: LeBron James, Cleveland Cavaliers

2007–08: Kobe Bryant, Los Angeles Lakers

2006–07: Dirk Nowitzki, Dallas Mavericks

2005–06: Steve Nash, Phoenix Suns

2004–05: Steve Nash, Phoenix Suns

2003–04: Kevin Garnett, Minnesota Timberwolves

2002–03: Tim Duncan, San Antonio Spurs

2001–02: Tim Duncan, San Antonio Spurs

2000–01: Allen Iverson, Philadelphia 76ers

1999–00: Shaquille O'Neal, Los Angeles Lakers

1998–99: Karl Malone, Utah Jazz

1997–98: Michael Jordan, Chicago Bulls

1996–97: Karl Malone, Utah Jazz

1995–96: Michael Jordan, Chicago Bulls

1994–95: David Robinson, San Antonio Spurs

1993–94: Hakeem Olajuwon, Houston Rockets

1992–93: Charles Barkley, Phoenix Suns

1991–92: Michael Jordan, Chicago Bulls

1990–91: Michael Jordan, Chicago Bulls

1989–90: Earvin Johnson, Los Angeles Lakers

1988–89: Earvin Johnson, Los Angeles Lakers

1987–88: Michael Jordan, Chicago Bulls

1986–87: Earvin Johnson, Los Angeles Lakers

1985–86: Larry Bird, Boston Celtics

1984–85: Larry Bird, Boston Celtics

1983–84: Larry Bird, Boston Celtics

1982–83: Moses Malone, Philadelphia 76ers

1981–82: Moses Malone, Houston Rockets

1980–81: Julius Erving, Philadelphia 76ers

1979–80: Kareem Abdul-Jabbar, Los Angeles Lakers

1978–79: Moses Malone, Houston Rockets

1977–78: Bill Walton, Portland Trail Blazers

1976–77: Kareem Abdul-Jabbar, Los Angeles Lakers

1975–76: Kareem Abdul-Jabbar, Los Angeles Lakers

1974–75: Bob McAdoo, Buffalo Braves

1973–74: Kareem Abdul-Jabbar, Milwaukee Bucks

1972–73: Dave Cowens, Boston Celtics

1971–72: Kareem Abdul-Jabbar, Milwaukee Bucks

1970–71: Kareem Abdul-Jabbar, Milwaukee Bucks

1969–70: Willis Reed, New York Knicks

1968–69: Wes Unseld, Baltimore Bullets

1967–68: Wilt Chamberlain, Philadelphia 76ers

1966–67: Wilt Chamberlain, Philadelphia 76ers

1965–66: Wilt Chamberlain, Philadelphia 76ers

1964–65: Bill Russell, Boston Celtics

1963–64: Oscar Robertson, Cincinnati Royals

1962–63: Bill Russell, Boston Celtics

1961–62: Bill Russell, Boston Celtics

1960–61: Bill Russell, Boston Celtics

1959–60: Wilt Chamberlain, Philadelphia Warriors

1958–59: Bob Pettit, St. Louis Hawks

1957–58: Bill Russell, Boston Celtics

1956–57: Bob Cousy, Boston Celtics

1955–56: Bob Pettit, St. Louis Hawks

NBA ALL-STAR GAME MVPs

2024–25: Stephen Curry, Golden State Warriors

2023–24: Damian Lillard, Milwaukee Bucks

2022–23: Jayson Tatum, Boston Celtics

2021–22: Stephen Curry, Golden State Warriors

2020–21: Giannis Antetokounmpo, Milwaukee Bucks

2019–20: Kawhi Leonard, Los Angeles Clippers

2018–19: Kevin Durant, Golden State Warriors

2017–18: LeBron James, Cleveland Cavaliers

2016–17: Anthony Davis, New Orleans Pelicans

2015–16: Russell Westbrook, Oklahoma City Thunder

2014–15: Russell Westbrook, Oklahoma City Thunder

2013–14: Kyrie Irving, Cleveland Cavaliers

2012–13: Chris Paul, Los Angeles Clippers

2011–12: Kevin Durant, Oklahoma City Thunder

2010–11: Kobe Bryant, Los Angeles Lakers

2009–10: Dwyane Wade, Miami Heat

2008–09: Shaquille O'Neal, Phoenix Suns (Tie)

2008–09: Kobe Bryant, Los Angeles Lakers (Tie)

2007–08: LeBron James, Cleveland Cavaliers

2006–07: Kobe Bryant, Los Angeles Lakers

2005–06: LeBron James, Cleveland Cavaliers

2004–05: Allen Iverson, Philadelphia 76ers

2003–04: Shaquille O'Neal, Los Angeles Lakers

2002–03: Kevin Garnett, Minnesota Timberwolves

2001–02: Kobe Bryant, Los Angeles Lakers

2000–01: Allen Iverson, Philadelphia 76ers

1999–00: Shaquille O'Neal, Los Angeles Lakers (Tie)

1999–00: Tim Duncan, San Antonio Spurs (Tie)

1997–98: Michael Jordan, Chicago Bulls

1996–97: Glen Rice, Charlotte Hornets

1995–96: Michael Jordan, Chicago Bulls

1994–95: Mitch Richmond, Sacramento Kings

1993–94: Scottie Pippen, Chicago Bulls

1992–93: John Stockton, Utah Jazz (Tie)

1992–93: Karl Malone, Utah Jazz (Tie)

1991–92: Earvin Johnson, Los Angeles Lakers

1990–91: Charles Barkley, Philadelphia 76ers

1989–90: Earvin Johnson, Los Angeles Lakers

1988–89: Karl Malone, Utah Jazz

1987–88: Michael Jordan, Chicago Bulls

1986–87: Tom Chambers, Seattle SuperSonics

1985–86: Isiah Thomas, Detroit Pistons

1984–85: Ralph Sampson, Houston Rockets

1983–84: Isiah Thomas, Detroit Pistons

1982–83: Julius Erving, Philadelphia 76ers

1981–82: Larry Bird, Boston Celtics

1980–81: Nate Archibald, Boston Celtics

1979–80: George Gervin, San Antonio Spurs

1978–79: David Thompson, Denver Nuggets

1977–78: Randy Smith, Buffalo Braves

1976–77: Julius Erving, Philadelphia 76ers

1975–76: Dave Bing, Washington Bullets

1974–75: Walt Frazier, New York Knicks

1973–74: Bob Lanier, Detroit Pistons

1972–73: Dave Cowens, Boston Celtics

1971–72: Jerry West, Los Angeles Lakers

1970–71: Lenny Wilkens, Seattle SuperSonics

1969–70: Willis Reed, New York Knicks

1968–69: Oscar Robertson, Cincinnati Royals

1967–68: Hal Greer, Philadelphia 76ers

1966–67: Rick Barry, San Francisco Warriors

1965–66: Adrian Smith, Cincinnati Royals

1964–65: Jerry Lucas, Cincinnati Royals

1963–64: Oscar Robertson, Cincinnati Royals

1962–63: Bill Russell, Boston Celtics

1961–62: Bob Pettit, St. Louis Hawks

1960–61: Oscar Robertson, Cincinnati Royals

1959–60: Wilt Chamberlain, Philadelphia Warriors

1958–59: Bob Pettit, St. Louis Hawks (Tie)

1958–59: Elgin Baylor, Minneapolis Lakers (Tie)

1957–58: Bob Pettit, St. Louis Hawks

1956–57: Bob Cousy, Boston Celtics

1955–56: Bob Pettit, St. Louis Hawks

1954–55: Bill Sharman, Boston Celtics

1953–54: Bob Cousy, Boston Celtics

1952–53: George Mikan, Minneapolis Lakers

1951–52: Paul Arizin, Philadelphia Warriors

1950–51: Ed Macauley, Boston Celtics

»NBA FINALS MVPs

2024–25: Shai Gilgeous-Alexander, Oklahoma City Thunder

2023–24: Jaylen Brown, Boston Celtics

2022–23: Nikola Jokic, Denver Nuggets

2021–22: Stephen Curry, Golden State Warriors

2020–21: Giannis Antetokounmpo, Milwaukee Bucks

2019–20: LeBron James, Los Angeles Lakers

2018–19: Kawhi Leonard, Toronto Raptors

2017–18: Kevin Durant, Golden State Warriors

2016–17: Kevin Durant, Golden State Warriors

2015–16: LeBron James, Cleveland Cavaliers

2014–15: Andre Iguodala, Golden State Warriors

2013–14: Kawhi Leonard, San Antonio Spurs

2012–13: LeBron James, Miami Heat

2011–12: LeBron James, Miami Heat

2010–11: Dirk Nowitzki, Dallas Mavericks

2009–10: Kobe Bryant, Los Angeles Lakers

2008–09: Kobe Bryant, Los Angeles Lakers

2007–08: Paul Pierce, Boston Celtics

2006–07: Tony Parker, San Antonio Spurs

2005–06: Dwyane Wade, Miami Heat

2004–05: Tim Duncan, San Antonio Spurs

2003–04: Chauncey Billups, Detroit Pistons

2002–03: Tim Duncan, San Antonio Spurs

2001–02: Shaquille O'Neal, Los Angeles Lakers

2000–01: Shaquille O'Neal, Los Angeles Lakers

1999–00: Shaquille O'Neal, Los Angeles Lakers

1998–99: Tim Duncan, San Antonio Spurs

1997–98: Michael Jordan, Chicago Bulls

1996–97: Michael Jordan, Chicago Bulls

1995–96: Michael Jordan, Chicago Bulls

1994–95: Hakeem Olajuwon, Houston Rockets

1993–94: Hakeem Olajuwon, Houston Rockets

1992–93: Michael Jordan, Chicago Bulls

1991–92: Michael Jordan, Chicago Bulls

1990–91: Michael Jordan, Chicago Bulls

1989–90: Isiah Thomas, Detroit Pistons

1988–89: Joe Dumars,
Detriot Pistons

1987–88: James Worthy,
Los Angeles Lakers

1986–87: Earvin Johnson,
Los Angeles Lakers

1985–86: Larry Bird,
Boston Celtics

1984–85: Kareem Abdul-Jabbar,
Los Angeles Lakers

1983–84: Larry Bird,
Boston Celtics

1982–83: Moses Malone,
Philadelphia 76ers

1981–82: Earvin Johnson,
Los Angeles Lakers

1980–81: Cedric Maxwell,
Boston Celtics

1979–80: Earvin Johnson,
Los Angeles Lakers

1978–79: Dennis Johnson,
Seattle SuperSonics

1977–78: Wes Unseld,
Washington Bullets

1976–77: Bill Walton,
Portland Trail Blazers

1975–76: Jo Jo White,
Boston Celtics

1974–75: Rick Barry,
Golden State Warriors

1973–74: John Havlicek,
Boston Celtics

1972–73: Willis Reed,
New York Knicks

1971–72: Wilt Chamberlain,
Los Angeles Lakers

1970–71: Kareem Abdul-Jabbar,
Milwaukee Bucks

1969–70: Willis Reed,
New York Knicks

1968–69: Jerry West,
Los Angeles Lakers

ACKNOWLEDGMENTS

Writing a book of any kind is a team effort, and I'd like to say thank-you to my editor on this project and others with Firefly Books, Julie Takasaki, for her thoroughness and patience through this process. In basketball terms, Julie is a great point guard. I'd also like to recognize every basketball writer's best friend: Basketball-Reference.com, the no-frills database that helps bring some statistical rigor to exercises like this one. I would also like to mention Spotrac.com, the source for much of the financial information used in this effort, as well as the treasure trove of data on NBA.com. The other sources are mentioned by name. As well, where players' quotes are not credited, they are taken from publicly available sources or from interviews I conducted personally. I'd also like to thank Rogers Sportsnet, which has enabled me to write and report on the Raptors and the NBA so thoroughly for all these years — I couldn't have a more supportive team. Finally, I'd like to thank my wife, Faeron, who has always been the backbone of our family throughout my career, as well as our now adult children, Avery and Ellis, who have been my inspiration so often for so many things.

Victor Wembanyama of the San Antonio Spurs shoots a three during a game against the Chicago Bulls on January 6, 2025.

PROFILE INDEX

PHOTO CREDITS

Associated Press

AP Photo/Aaron Gash: 53
AP Photo/Abbie Parr: 42, 61, 88, 114
AP Photo/Adam Hunger: 136
AP Photo/Alan Youngblood: 145
AP Photo/Ashley Landis: 43, 111, 113, 147
AP Photo/Charles Krupa: 85, 129, 138, 149
AP Photo/Chris Szagola: 48, 81, 110, 146, 148
AP Photo/Darren Abate: 40–41, 47, 103
AP Photo/David J. Phillip: 98–99
AP Photo/David Zalubowski: 26, 28, 90, 91, 141
AP Photo/Duane Burleson: 15, 59, 104
AP Photo/Ed Betz: 33
AP Photo/Eric Gay: 13, 73
AP Photo/Frank Franklin II: 75, 131
AP Photo/George Walker IV: 87
AP Photo/Godofredo A. Vásquez: 44
AP Photo/Jeff Chiu: 17, 83, 112
AP Photo/Jeffrey Phelps: 10–11
AP Photo/Jessie Alcheh: 124–25
AP Photo/John Munson: 76
AP Photo/John Raoux: 144
AP Photo/Julio Cortez: 5, 68
AP Photo/Kyle Phillips: 29, 57
AP Photo/Kyusung Gong: 19
AP Photo/Marcio Jose Sanchez: 36, 126
AP Photo/Mark J. Terrill: 51, 58, 133, 134
AP Photo/Marta Lavandier: 143
AP Photo/Mary Altaffer: 38
AP Photo/Matt Krohn: 50, 80, 117
AP Photo/Matt Slocum: 23, 74
AP Photo/Michael Conroy: 107, 108, 132, 137, 142
AP Photo/Michael Dwyer: 30, 139
AP Photo/Nate Billings: 24, 25, 78, 79, 92
AP Photo/Nell Redmond: 116
AP Photo/Nic Coury: 16
AP Photo/Nick Wass: 46, 54, 100, 101
AP Photo/Pamela Smith: 84, 121
AP Photo/Phelan M. Ebenhack: 106, 115
AP Photo/Rick Scuteri: 12, 14, 20, 21, 35, 86, 109, 119, 135, 140
AP Photo/Ron Schwane, File: 64
AP Photo/Steve Dykes: 77
AP Photo/Sue Ogrocki: 55
AP Photo/Tony Avelar: 63
AP Photo/Tony Gutierrez: 123
Carlos Avila Gonzalez/San Francisco Chronicle via AP: 66, 82
Europa Press via AP: 34
Scott Strazzante/San Francisco Chronicle via AP: 9, 70–71, 89

Getty Images

David Alvarez / NBAE: 62
Julien Bacot/BAL / NBAE: 96
SUZANNE CORDEIRO / AFP: 95

Icon Sportswire

Icon Sportswire: 93
Melissa Tamez/Icon Sportswire: 6, 18, 22, 27, 31, 45, 49, 52, 56, 60, 72, 93, 102, 105, 118, 130, 157

Also from Firefly Books

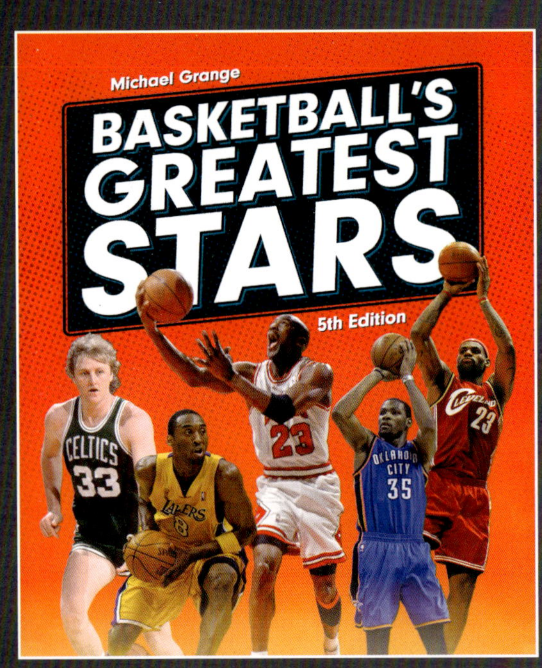

Basketball's Greatest Stars, 5th Edition

By Michael Grange

Basketball's Greatest Stars takes you courtside for a look at the 50 best players in NBA history. From the early days of Bob Cousy to the Showtime era of Magic Johnson, from Michael Jordan's electrifying dunks to LeBron James' all-out dominance — the legends are here! Relive the moments and revel in the triumphs of the NBA's greatest superstars, including Kareem Abdul-Jabbar, Larry Bird, Stephen Curry, Wilt Chamberlain, Shaquille O'Neal, Oscar Robertson, Kevin Durant, and many more.

This fifth edition also contains a new crop of 15 stars who are dominating today's game and could one day reach the heights of Basketball's Greatest, including Luka Doncic, Jayson Tatum, Shai Gilgeous-Alexander and Donovan Mitchell.

Jam-packed with unforgettable stories, mind-blowing stats and over 120 photos that capture the on-court excitement, *Basketball's Greatest Stars* is the ultimate book for every NBA fan.

NBA 75

By Dave Zarum

NBA 75 tells the story of the NBA, all 75 years — from its early barnstorming days to the multibillion-dollar sports league it is today.

Readers are treated to all the biggest moments and greatest superstars, with over 75 stories ranging from Jerry West's 33-win streak Lakers, through Jordan's repeat three-peat Bulls, to Steph Curry and the 73-win Warriors and beyond. But this retrospective doesn't shy away from the league's controversies, covering its struggles with racial bigotry, Magic Johnson's HIV diagnosis, Len Bias' tragic draft-night death and the cocaine-fuelled late seventies when the Finals were broadcast on tape delay.

Each story is fully illustrated with iconic photos and accompanied by stat boxes and side stories of some of the Association's more curious and overlooked moments.

NBA 75 is the definitive guide to the history of the NBA — perfect for any fan who wants to learn more about the league they love or simply catch up on what they've been missing.

Available wherever books are sold.